Go Fly a Kite!

Ten Surprising Strategies for Success in Your Homeschool

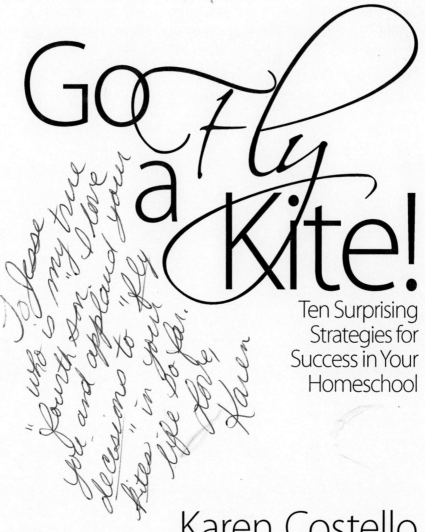

To please — who is my true "fourth son," I love you and applaud your decision to "fly kites" in your life so far. Love, Karen

Karen Costello

Table of Contents

Chapter 1: CREATE 1

Chapter 2: PRAY and *then* plan! 11

Chapter 3: READ 25

Chapter 4: MEMORIZE 31

Chapter 5: SIMPLIFY 37

Chapter 6: GROW 55

Chapter 7: APPRECIATE 67

Chapter 8: SERVE 79

Chapter 9: LAUGH 85

Chapter 10: FIGHT 115

Forward

Although I have wanted to write this book, I have never felt adequate, but this letter from my husband helped me give it to God.

> K-
> You are a home education expert. Not based on theories. Not based on popularity. Not based on recognition. Based on results.
>
> You and I both would be quick to credit God for our children's growth, development, and accomplishments. However, we must be willing to follow God's guidance, love mightily, discipline with courage and mercy, explore all possibilities to tailor each child's training, work extremely hard to incorporate as much exposure as possible to find each child's passion, etc., etc., etc.
>
> You have excelled in all these areas and much more. You must write a book to guide the current homeschoolers and the next generations. A timeless guide to raising and training children. Not a trendy book dealing with passing fads and changing curriculum. A book that would share your hopes, dreams, prayers, philosophies, and efforts. How you modeled leadership, service, godliness, and sacrifice.

It might be difficult to write such a book without seeming arrogant. Therefore, you should interview other successful homeschoolers nationwide to discover their truths and secrets to success. Your book could be a compilation of many families who produced godly, productive children. The book could be like a favorite recipes cookbook. Those with little knowledge could follow your "recipes" for training children. There are ingredients that you take for granted or assume that others would be clueless about.

You are the most qualified person I know to write this book. No one has significantly more experience. Arguably, no one has more "proof in the pudding." This book could and should bring glory to God. The timing is perfect. Prior to now, there hasn't been enough data, you haven't had time, and you hadn't finished your pudding. People hunger for truth from someone who has walked the walk. No one has walked it better.

I believe in you and love you,
T

I dedicate this book to the mothers of my grandchildren and future great-grandchildren as they seek to fly against the pressures of this conformist world and truly soar above all expectations. I want to thank my "book doula", Lisa Grimenstein, and my contributing friends Colleen Whitver, Anita Doughty, Ginger McCreery, LeDonna Scalf, Elizabeth Martin, Gloria Merritt, Anne Ryun, and Mandy Anders. I could never have written this without the patience of our son Gil, and the incredible encouragement of my husband Tim.

When his pager beeped, the captain of the Warriors boys' varsity basketball team forgot every play and strategy for that important tournament game and ran off to the players' bench. He joined his younger brother, another starting player, there, and together in their sweat-soaked uniforms they ran toward the exit door.

Instead of being outraged, their coach and fans smiled and actually cheered, for they all knew the secret: those two young men had been summoned to a miracle. They were literally racing against time to witness the birth of their baby brother. Thoughts of a championship trophy were replaced by those of a much greater prize. They joined their sister and, half an hour later, from the back edge of a hospital room, saw their younger brother, Luke, draw his first breath.

The bonding experience that began in that little room was echoed a few months later. My 19-year-old son, Will, was watching his baby brother sleep in my arms and said, almost wistfully (if a teenage boy can *be* wistful), "Can we freeze this moment in time?" As any mom can tell you, that is impossible. But as a homeschool mom, those precious "Mary-pondered-these-things-in-her-heart" moments can be crystallized. Those moments comprise what this book hopes to put down as a piece of living history.

Although any family's history is subject to faulty memory, incomplete data, and revisionist thinking, my desire is to encourage all who read this to realize that amazing relationships can spring out of following God's calling. And if you gather little bits of wisdom and insight in the process, even better. In the attempt to chronicle the heritage handed down to me, I hope to show how each member of our family boldly fought against the common culture to make a difference in our lives, both now and eternally.

In the early 1980s, families across America were hearing the same call to a revolutionary way of thinking—a radical reinvention of how families operate—and a call to self-sacrifice.

In sharing my family history, I hope to show how God prepared us for just such a time.

Most every worthwhile homeschool experience develops through trial and error. There is no "one size fits all" formula to guarantee success. But there are certain elements which should be included in every home education process.

It is my prayer that incorporating these ten simple strategies will enable you to reach heights you can only imagine—that these ten verbs will challenge you to venture into the not-so-scary unknown. That these ten dynamics will propel you forward into God's great plan—and let you SOAR LIKE A KITE!

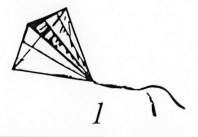

1

Create

"It is the supreme art of the teacher to awaken joy in creative expression and knowledge."

—Albert Einstein

One of the simplest yet most enjoyable elements of home-schooling is that of creating fun memories. All families can and do create memories, whether intentional or not—but, upon evaluation, are they significant? We homeschoolers have the distinct advantage of *quality time* to invest in creating these memories—and a God-given responsibility to do so.

When you invest twenty-five years in a vocation, you not only have experience, but perspective. As I think about the hundreds of families we have known through homeschooling, the healthiest ones are those who know how to create joy together. Whether through shared interests, ministries, or work, they delight in making a difference as a family. One way is through creating or re-playing dramatic presentations.

Colleen, a mother of a homeschooled National Merit Scholar finalist, says:

Life without live drama is no life at all. We did our own literary festivals with friends, drama camps, and amateur theatre
that were a part of academic drama class. I think one of the
saddest losses for the child whose life is regulated by a frantic
schedule of activities is the loss of time to dream and think
and play in the half-fantasy, half-real world that children create
when they are allowed to do it. Too many children plug into an
electronic substitute and become obsessed with that. We were
able to host our literary festivals at a nearby botanical garden
for two or three years. Around fifteen families took blankets,
lawn chairs, and picnic lunches to an area beside a lovely lake.
We let the margin of the lake be our stage for the skits and
monologues that the students had prepared. Preschoolers and
seniors in high school and all ages in between entertained us
with Milne, Shakespeare, Stoppard, Lewis Carroll, nursery
rhymes, Twain. Most had on costumes to match their parts. We
had a lush spring day and the spirit of friendship to make the
day even more special.

*"Creative recreation, in my personal definition, can be
thought of in two ways. Firstly, it is recreation which produces
creativity, refreshes one's ideas and stirs one to 'produce.' Sec-
ondly, it is recreation which is the result of original ideas, creative because someone has creatively planned an evening, a day,
and an occupation which in itself is fresh and different."*
—Edith Schaeffer

Play-acting and drama offer many opportunities for success and self-confidence. Wendy, from Georgia, states about her
school day: "My daughter especially loved to dress up and pre-
tend. I think the early role-playing gave my children confidence
to attempt many activities later."

Creating memories is much more than an early-childhood
activity. So many families are devastated when their children
become teenagers and they never see them again. My husband
and I felt the importance of making friends of our children—be-

cause children *want* to spend time with their friends! With that in mind, we created many family traditions designed to enhance our family heritage.

One such tradition, which has stood the test of time, is our Sunday lunch. The components are simple: a home-cooked lunch, dessert, and a question for all to respond to—and more importantly, for all the rest of us to *listen* to. It is so important to create a safe place where each person can be heard. My husband, Tim, added an addition to our house for one main purpose: to enlarge our dining room to contain all our children and their spouses. Many Sundays, we have our entire family, their closest friends, and a few "extra" visitors from church. Although Sundays at the Costello house are quite eventful, the work that makes them so special begins on Saturdays. In addition to making dessert, picking up the house, and running to the grocery store, we spend many Saturdays busily attending family basketball games, hosting sleepovers, and volunteering for family projects.

Below is a journal excerpt from a typical, recent Sunday.

> At 5:30 I had to get up to start the chicken pot pies—we need 4 for the numbers we usually have for Sunday lunch. While I was making a pecan-vinaigrette dressing for our salad, we got a phone call from a Sunday school teacher saying that she could not be there, and would I substitute [this happens once a month for some class]. This meant gathering crafts, snacks, and a lesson, so I nixed plans for another vegetable, deciding to open a big can of peaches instead.
> Sunday school is always unpredictable—Rob keeps me laughing! Worship was especially great—many people gave testimonies of God's unbelievably abundant blessings. We had several people recovering (and delivered!) from addictions; Clayton [my son–in–law] told of God meeting specific and timely monetary needs for his family; and Stevone told of the Christmas at their house that would not have happened without God's generosity.
> I then rushed home to heat up the pies, set the table and get tea ready....We all eat dinner (which, by the way, is the Southern word for lunch).... The after-dinner question that day is: Who

are you most like: your mom or your dad? We had a great discussion and then moved into the great room to visit and do the puzzles in the Sunday paper. Gil, Scott and Cheyenne take all the young boys outside to play basketball—and because they just *can't* get enough, they all go to the rec center and play BB for two more hours.

By the time I get all the dishes cleaned up, it is time to start the beef stew for the young couples' marriage class, which starts at 5:30. I called to check on one of our favorite couples in the world: Papa Schu and Marie. He turns 91 this May and is still active in serving at church, using his spiritual gift of encouragement in *every* situation, and taking care of his wife of 60+ years who has Alzheimer's. He *hates* accepting help, but I could tell he was sooo tired, and when I asked if I could do anything, such as bring over supper, and he ACCEPTED (!), I knew he was having a hard day. I visited for a few minutes and just barely got home before the first couples arrived....

There is always great food, much laughter...and babies literally everywhere.

....Tonight, Tim leads the group in evaluating how we treat our spouses as friends. These couples...are such a tightly-knit group and give each other much wise counsel. We try to wrap it up by 7:30, but usually we all hang out until kiddoes' bedtimes.

What a FULL Sunday! On days like this, I hit the bed, exhausted. And guess what? When I'm tempted to feel as if I'll never have my energy back, a good night's sleep is all I need! The point is that God will faithfully provide energy for the tasks He has called you to complete. Creating significant and intentional memories is well worth being "spent for."

Even on a single Sunday, our family creates so many memories—memories of fun events celebrated together. We love to host large parties, and, with that in mind, we have gradually designed an entire park-like setting in the woods on our property, with a treehouse, zipline, playhouse, waterfall, stage, dance floor, and "fire circle," which is surrounded by a circular bench that seats twenty-five people. These woods have hosted weddings, engagements, band nights, countless youth group and church devotionals, dances, service club bonfires, outdoor concerts, every holiday you can imagine, and ceremonies for sports and Scouts. Yearly, we host a university social organization's initiation bonfire and their subsequent dinner celebration. We hosted our son's Eagle Scout ceremony, where we roasted a pig in a firepit overnight and then served BBQ to four hundred people the next day.

You might think that all this hosting would keep me very busy cleaning and decorating, but my motto has always been to give two big parties back-to-back so that I only have to clean once! This simplifies my life in so many ways because I can reuse the same table arrangements, flowers, left-over paper goods, and extra chairs. Our neighbors frequently see hundreds of cars pull into our driveway on two consecutive nights (we have GREAT neighbors).

As you can see, we've created many special family traditions, and continue to do so. I believe it's important that you create your own personal family traditions that strengthen your beliefs, your sense of belonging, and your family's attitude of "teamwork." These traditions should be meaningful, consistent, and fun. There are innumerable ways to create meaningful memories and family traditions. Volumes have been written on the subject. But my hope is that, as homeschoolers, we can use these traditions as a way to enrich our time together. In traveling and speaking to homeschoolers, I am continually amazed at their creativity in instituting significant family traditions.

Many of these traditions revolve around travel. I know of families who bike or hike together. One family from Indiana made a years-long study of the Civil War and planned their vacations around camping at all the major battlefields. Our family loved camping, and we still share stories of getting lost on hiking trails for miles, waking up to three inches of water *in* our tents, and the time Dad cooked an entire chicken by covering it in mud and burying it in coals! (It was incredibly good, by the way.) We also love going yearly to one specific beach in Florida—and doing essentially the *same* things each time we are there. Some of these early traditions have changed with time—I used to cook almost every vacation meal in our condo (finances dictated!), but now the married couples each get a night to cook for everyone else—guys included! We always eat at our special restaurant, we always play games, we always play golf or tennis, we always boogie-board, and we always go thrift-store shopping. The "always" is key here—the consistent effort to incorporate that which brings the family closer.

Many families create their traditions around food: Saturday morning chocolate chip pancakes, Friday night pizza, Seder meal celebrations, a special apple-wine dessert every Christmas Eve, bread baking, lasagna on Thanksgiving. Discover the foods of your particular heritage. Celebrate your study of other cultures with international meal nights. Many families cook together and involve *each* family member in a meaningful way. The important thing is to attempt to make it consistent and enjoyable.

A Midwest homeschooling mom of two remembers "going to visit a 100-year-old castle, creating a castle out of large cardboard boxes in a friend's backyard, and having a Renaissance-period feast with period food and costumes." Traditions like this have helped her children grow up to be incredibly inventive and creative in their jobs today.

Homeschool moms are masters at creating fun out of everyday experiences. One resourceful mom gives this advice:

> Keep a set of clean "creek clothes and shoes" in a plastic bag in the car. This way we would be able to stop at a creek when opportunity presented itself, and I was prepared for the boys to have a great science lesson. They loved to check out pond scum and to collect rocks and "treasures." We would take home the rocks and "treasures" (old nails, Happy Meal toys, Matchbox cars, etc.). I never had to ask them to look up the rocks in a book—it was something *they* asked to do. We would have fun in the water and then change back into dry clothes and put the wet clothes in the plastic bag to wash when we got home (I would love to have had Croc shoes back then!). I was glad for all the cheap pairs of tennis shoes I could buy at yard sales. We all loved those science field trips.

In many ways other than food, it is important to simply learn about and celebrate your heritage. When our family celebrates our heritage, we have much for which to be thankful. My mother-in-law, who was killed in a car wreck years ago, was a major influence on our entire family. She instilled the character I see today in my husband. Her influence on our oldest three children is amazing. She created beauty and wealth-of-living experiences in everything she undertook. There are many things I've learned from Jean Costello, for she taught through how she lived and served.

All who knew Tim's mom would characterize her as the Proverb 31 woman. She was the oldest of five children and grew up in Athens, Alabama. Her parents, Herman and Reba, were the most industrious, loyal, humble Christians, and taught all their children how to serve others. Herman was a carpenter/chicken farmer, while Reba was the epitome of a Christian homemaker. Betty Jean was so loved by her siblings that it was noted at her funeral that she had never had a cross word with anyone. Her fighting spirit had nothing to do with an innate desire to win. Instead, she created and fought to keep her family well clothed and fed, and especially worked to instill in them a strong Christian heritage.

Her own mother had taught her more than the basics of cooking, harvesting, preserving, and sewing: she taught her the concept of true service to her family. Although Jean once said that she would never marry a teacher or a preacher, she loved her preacher/professor husband faithfully until her death in 1994. She typed his thesis, made him lunch every day, did their taxes (to the penny!), and offered her lap to him when he came home from school to take a nap after lunch each day. She creatively worked to give him the best of her daily life. She fought to keep four children fed and clothed on a preacher's salary. She made all their clothes—even the boys' suits! She consistently made memories on frequent trips to Alabama—certainly for all holidays, but for harvesting crops as well. She hosted family Sunday lunches and Costello Christmases, loving any excuse to get everyone together.

She stayed connected with her entire family. She wrote to her mother faithfully—many times simply chronicling how many quarts of jam and green beans she had canned. She called her daughters-in-law daily—just to check in—but also to offer whatever was needed. Because she wasted nothing and preserved all the foods she grew (or was given!), she had a huge basement full of canned goods, and two deep freezers full of preserved foods. When any of the family was struggling financially, she offered unconditionally what was needed.

Her heart was tuned to the Lord. She was content to remain in the background, serve others, and never get any credit. For years, she would take either lunch or dinner (or sometimes both) to a sister-in-law who was struggling with MS. She cooked, cleaned, and helped to parent her sister-in-law's children. She did nothing to give herself glory, but always gave the glory to the Lord. She taught Sunday school, never missed ladies' Bible class, and faithfully studied the scriptures.

She lived her entire life for ideals which were important to her—the church, her family, David Lipscomb University—by saving, cooking, preserving, sewing, and creating beauty. She exhibited the love of creation in all she accomplished. Her life is a testimony to the worthiness of fighting for what is important.

As I reflect on the marvelous heritage I've been given, I feel responsible to pass on godly insights which were taught to me. Faithful testimonies of those who have gone before us should encourage us to pour out our lives in service to others—especially to our children. The lessons learned from past generations can inspire us to create our own exciting personal histories.

I love the concept of creating unit studies. This educational choice is ideal for uniting, rather than dividing families. It is important to study one topic on each child's different level, because we do not *have* to bring the schoolroom home. We have the freedom to delve into each child's interests and cover what will benefit them later. My children remember fondly the building of an inner ear, the medieval festival, and the dissection of a cow eyeball—because we did it all *together*. At the end of this chapter is an incomplete list of unit study ideas to give you a springboard for your own family based on their interests.

As you plan your unit of study, it would be beneficial to incorporate correlating field trips with your family. We have a small group of families who meet one afternoon a week to do projects, character lessons, and field trips. One important note, however: the larger the group, the *less* effective educational instruction! We have found (through trial and error) that four to six families are ideal—any more and the kids would rather visit than learn.

Flexibility is critical in creating these educational opportunities. Kerri, from California, loves the flexibility inherent in home education. Because her husband has an erratic work schedule, she incorporates homeschooling on an as-needed basis. One year she homeschooled all three of her children while moving cross-country. The next year she only homeschooled the youngest. She loves field trips and tries to incorporate her children who are in school into her field trips as much as possible.

Anita, from Iowa, also appreciates flexibility: "So much of our schooling went on in the car. They were captive. I thank God for Discovery toys and Little Bear educational tapes playing in the car. They loved the hands-on stuff and were just happy to be occupied."

Creation is the first recorded description of how God works. It is such a privilege to be invited by Him to join Him in creating. Enjoy the freedom homeschooling provides to CREATE beauty, joy, and lasting memories.

Unit Study Ideas

Caves	Dinosaurs	Earthquakes
Fossils	Glaciers	Volcanoes
Rocks	Birds	Human Body Systems
Insects	Reptiles	Invertebrates
Marine Life	Mammals	Marsupials
Spiders	Weather	Hurricanes
NASA	Solar System	Simple Machines
Inventions	Flight	Archaeology
Vikings	Medieval	Explorers
Nations	Maps and Flags	Australia
Alaska	Switzerland	Japan
Mexico	Africa	Theater
Classical Composers	Thanksgiving	Christmas
Nutrition	Teeth	Anatomy
Farming	Pyramids	Pets
Poisonous Creatures	Electricity	Military Heroes
Rainbows and Refraction	Energy	Plants
Ancestry	Light	Native Americans
Declaration of Independence	Earth's Crust	Messiah
Mummies	Plagues	Musical Terms
Needlework	Letter Writing	Ancient Greece
Ancient Rome	Braille	Poetry
Industrial Revolution	Photography	Computers
Covenant	Sports	Jamestown
Lewis and Clark	Manners	Olympics
Jerusalem	Judicial Branch	Ten Commandments
Trail of Tears	Pulleys	Telephone
Hawaii	Sundials	The White House
Deserts	Scorpions	Monarchy
Fire Safety	Carpentry	Printing Press
Kites	Apples	Laura Ingalls Wilder

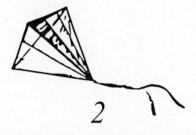

2

Pray

and *then* plan!

"All I have seen teaches me to trust the Creator for all I have not seen."

—Ralph Waldo Emerson

I was born 3-4-56. My birthday is March 4th....or MARCH FORTH. This pretty well sums up my approach to life: actively step out, go forward, and do it *now*. I am not in the minority as far as homeschoolers go. When I speak to large audiences, I frequently ask how many are first-born like me, or how many would characterize themselves as "type A" people. You would be amazed at the large percentage who are. The only reason I am not more surprised is that in order to homeschool, one must be willing to go against the popular culture—to be self-motivated—to be different. Another unifying factor in homeschoolers is the desire to be in control. We understand limitations in other forms of education, and we want to control the environment, the curricula, and the access to teaching. Because we are somewhat in charge, it can be easy to forget Who actually holds the key to everything. And because we are, for the most part, self-disciplined hard workers, we can quickly put an educational plan in place without sufficiently consulting the Giver of all good things.

I always advise new homeschoolers to pick a day (preferably in the first of summer), find a babysitter, and go to their church or library to spend some time alone reflecting on the task before them. Pray for each child, and listen to the Lord. Often, He gives me specific insights and character traits that He wants me to help mold in the coming school year. I'll then find what I intend to be that child's yearly verse (or passage). In addition to me having them memorize it, this helps the child to know exactly what our character emphasis will be, and serves as a great reminder at year's end of God's faithfulness in transforming us.

Only after this time would I *ever* be concerned with academic curricula. Too often, we major on the textbooks, which are only our *tools* for accomplishing God's purposes. We need to take our jobs seriously (but not ourselves!). Planning is incredibly important, but it must take a backseat to prayer.

My planning is two-part: I take an entire day in the summer—pack a plastic milk crate with all the books I'll need and a bag lunch—and go to an empty church classroom with two or three close friends. There, the rule is NO TALKING until lunch—I simply plan, in a "big picture" way, what I will teach during the first semester. I keep one journal with all the children's weeks broken down into subjects. At lunch, there is much discussion, but also much effort *not* to compare learning styles or texts. The length of my day depends on the number of children I'm teaching that year.

The second part of my overall planning takes place each Sunday afternoon, and that involves *weekly* lesson plans. This typically should not take too long—just mapping out how many pages per subject per day (or week). The only other time-consuming planning that I do during the year is right after Christmas, before I start the second half of the year. That is the time to re-evaluate the first semester and re-number what needs to be covered before the end of the year. This is why you should *never* plan the entire school year at first—your schedule will definitely change and will need to be altered. Pray first and then plan— with a *purpose.*

Gloria, from Colorado, when asked what she chose as her one activity in a rushed day, answered:

> Bible time! Mostly, it was in the form of reading passages, chatting a bit about them, trying to keep the kids focused, and then being on our knees to pray for God's grace to get it all done. I smile now to think that my oldest kids' common theme in their prayers was "Lord, help us to have a good day." My younger children now focus more on thankfulness and a realization of God's love in their prayers. My older ones were more works oriented and performance based. Hmmm—quite insightful!

In planning and setting goals, people who want to know God's will for them will immerse themselves in God's word and find delight in discovering how God thinks and what God wants. Isaiah 48:17 says, "I am the Lord your God who teaches you what is best for you—who directs you in *the way you should go*" (emphasis mine). There was a recent Tombstone® pizza commercial which made a cute play on words using the question homeschoolers—and everyone—should be asking themselves: "What do you want on *your* Tombstone?" I love Elisabeth Eliot's quote: "My whole life is an offering back to Him of all that I am and all that He wants me to be."

In setting goals, you need to take into account short-, medium-, and long-range aspirations. Short-range goals would be your daily lesson plans, while medium-range would include weekly and monthly plans. Long-range goals would be those character traits that are developed over a year or even a lifetime.

There needs to be a specific way of evaluating whether or not you have reached your goals. Lesson plans are simple and can be checked off. Medium-range goals can be evaluated through written or oral tests. However, long-range goals are much harder to evaluate. Some long-range evaluation tools we have used include recitals, end-of-year presentations, show-and-tell programs, a medieval festival, and a formal banquet showcasing an etiquette unit study.

There is a story about three little boys who lived up north. After another large snowfall, the father decided to try to relieve the children's boredom and offered a reward to the child who could walk the straightest line to him in the snow. The oldest, cautious one went first and decided to put one foot in front of the other. He never looked up and continued to carefully place one boot on the front tip of the previously stepped boot. When he finally looked up, he realized he was several feet off course, so he adjusted his path and made it to his father.

The middle child saw that his oldest brother was not going to win and decided to take a different approach. He decided to walk backwards, thinking to himself, *I'll watch where I've been. That way I will know exactly where I've been, so I will know exactly how to walk in a straight line.* Of course, this utterly failed. But the youngest son never looked down, looked in his father's face, and ran straight to him.

We can learn a lot from this illustration. We can focus so much on what is immediately in front of us that we fail to see life in the larger perspective. Or we can be so focused on what is past that we have no idea what is ahead. In a broader analogy, we need to look straight into our Father's face, and not let anything keep us from running to Him.

Your job as a homeschool parent is to set high goals—goals so high that you cannot reach them without God's help. You need to make sure each child understands his secure position in Jesus. Each child needs to know that he finds great favor in your eyes. Our children knew our love was unconditional but they were also able to realize that their hard work paid off in many success-es. God calls us to love Him with all our heart, soul, mind, and strength: a life devoted to Him will be an exceptional one. Each child must realize the importance of obedience, integrity, and honor. Lastly, each child must be given the opportunity for many success experiences. Your overall goal should be to match your child's talent to their passion. Find out what "sparks" them—what interests them.

When we began this journey twenty-five years ago, we wrote down what we wanted to see when we had finished training each child. And this is what I wrote as an all-encompassing vision: "An independent, obedient, self-motivated, dependable, considerate citizen who loves learning and has a heart to serve Jesus." This statement is so rich, so complicated, and so overwhelmingly difficult to implement.

Because I believe all children are gifted by God, and because I believe homeschool parents can easily step into the trap of comparing other children's progresses with their own, I will try to minimize tales of my own children. However, I think it is important to watch how God answers your specific prayers and goals concerning your children. I would like to break down each character trait that we wanted to see in our children and show how God has faithfully worked that out in each child. When I show an incident which truly illustrates that principle, I am going to term it as "the proof of the pudding," or "**POP.**"

Independent

So many of us have read James Dobson's *The Strong-Willed Child*, and we do recognize many of those outlined traits in our children—specifically in our first-borns! I *want* a strong-willed child—one who will be strong enough to obey me when I am not around. We wanted a child who would be willing to stand alone and do the right thing (like Daniel, who our daughter, Danielle, is partly named after). We never want to create students who are totally dependent on us, but those who work consistently toward being independent of us.

When we started homeschooling in 1983, we *had* to stand alone—not only because home-schooling was illegal, but because our families were not certain what this was all about. And who could blame them? Within our two families, we had *two* doctorates in education (one taught university education majors for forty years), a teacher/coach and a school superintendent. There were absolutely no role models in our generation to point to as successes in homeschooling. We were pretty arrogant in our explanation of our plans and were met with much skepticism. This taught us to learn to be more vulnerable and to make independence a major goal in our children's lives. When your decisions are held up to ridicule, you are forced to redefine your purpose and *be* refined in the process.

The other side to being independent is to expect your children to sometimes make choices that are different from what you would do. After all, we are training them to *not* go along with the status quo! When both our boys went through their "long-hair" phase, it irked me that they would choose that over my preferred conservative look for them. But they were both incredibly respectful, and we decided that the issue was not important enough to fight about. And it *was* a short phase!

POP: We were without TV for about ten years. When the kids went to the grandparents' house, of course all they wanted to do was watch cartoons. One such afternoon, Tim's mom said she had been watching TV with them and had dozed off. She woke up to six-year-old Will turning off the TV. When questioned why, he said, "Well, there was this show that I know Mom wouldn't want us to watch. And you were asleep, so I just turned it off."

Obedient
Early on, Tim taught all our children the true meaning of obedience—to obey IMMEDIATELY and COMPLETELY. If, after being told to do a chore, a child says, "In a minute," they would be punished for disobedience. Besides understanding that

God expects our obedience, this was an object lesson concerning safety. Here is the example we used: we would teach them that if they did not learn to obey immediately, and there was a car coming straight toward them and one of us said, "Run toward me!" there could be tragic consequences for not obeying immediately. Too many children of this generation are allowed to question their parents—as in "How come?" or "Why?" If this hesitation and questioning of parental command happened in this situation, they could be killed.

The *complete* aspect of obedience is very important also. If a child performed a chore *almost* completely, they would either forfeit the reward or be punished. Too often, we give our children too much grace and thus teach them that "close enough" is the same as completion. Of course, that is ridiculous.

POP: We could not have known then that the vocations our children were destined for were so exacting. Will, as a doctor and anesthesiologist, is held to the minutest forms of exactness. Gil, in public accounting for three years, knew his very job depended on exact completion on all his audits. As a nurse, Danielle was responsible for oncology/hematology patients—some of whom were completing bone marrow transplants. They each had to totally understand what "complete and immediate obedience" entailed.

Self-motivated

As parents, we desired for our children to obey—to please God and to please us—but there was more. We wanted our children to develop an intrinsic desire to grow. We have seen homeschool families that actually never homeschooled in the same room. They were given assignments to complete and were told to report back to Mom when they were finished. This certainly did not increase family unity (or cause fun memories of homeschool!). After assignments were done, they were finished.

Our desire is that our children would learn to set goals, carry them out, and then evaluate the results. We started with small experiments (as in completing a reading list before eating out at a special restaurant), and progressed to the children actually being responsible for important projects. For example, they were entrusted to incubate chicken eggs, raise the chicks, and then sell dozens of eggs to friends. At different times, the kids sold to-mato plants, managed a carwash, and rebuilt a 1952 Plymouth.

POP: Danielle began taking violin lessons when she was seven (by the way, the *perfect* age to start any lessons!). We chose the Suzuki method, but with an added emphasis on learning to read music much earlier than a traditional Suzuki student would. At around age thirteen, she became weary and a little bored of the instrument. We encouraged her to continue practicing, but we were open to ideas on how we could continue to make it fun for her. She had heard of an electric violin, and was intrigued by it. So, she began also playing this new instrument. Because this was her idea, she felt ownership in mastering it. Subsequently, she bought her own cello, taught herself to play it, went to college on a partial music scholarship, and played on music videos and on a band tour across America. To this day, her favorite down-time activity is being alone and playing her instruments.

Dependable

I believe dependability is more closely "caught than taught." Children will see this (or the lack of) in your life so clearly—and they will call you on it! If I sign on to teach Sunday school for a quarter, I had better be there—on time. Teaching your children about dependability involves setting clear boundaries on priori-ties. Every time one of our children signs up for sports, inevita-bly a practice will interfere with church activities. We have rare-ly allowed our kids to skip church for a sports event—certainly not a practice. We understand the importance of commitment to a team, but the bigger message is the one we send our kids—that going to church is more important than any sports team.

We had a long period in our boys' lives when it seemed as if we were sending the wrong message about being dependable. There are many worthwhile activities in which young boys can be involved. Due to our family preferences, we decided that being in Boy Scouts was worth sacrificing our time, money, and energy. Our boys also discovered how much they loved sports— especially basketball. In a school setting, it would be fairly impossible to achieve the highest ranking in scouting—Eagle Scout—and be a starter on a varsity sports team at the same time. The time constraints and the weekend scheduling are almost diametrically opposed—both your coach and your scoutmaster want most of your weekends!

POP: Because both boys were greatly motivated to achieve the highest level in both Scouts and varsity sports, we decided to help them reach their goals. Tim was very involved in both— he served as the president of our basketball board and rarely missed a Scout meeting. We were blessed to have a wonderful basketball coach and a scoutmaster who was driven to excellence. However, Tim's motto at that point in our lives became: "We cannot please both men all the time, so we will be content to make each of them equally miserable." I write this in jest, but there was much truth to the practical, weekend juxtaposition of activities. Each man desired *total* participation, but each would have to be happy with shared leadership from our boys. Both boys did achieve Eagle Scout status, and both boys excelled in varsity sports. Each served as captains of their teams, and one was recruited by several Christian universities to play college basketball. Their dedication to succeed and to be dependable propelled them through an incredibly hard schedule.

Considerate
If you homeschool your children through high school, and they are unkind, you might as well have not bothered. One thing I have noticed is that Christian families are allowing sibling ri-

valry—excusing it and even justifying it. This is anathema in a homeschool family. You are around each other 24/7, and you cannot permit that sort of behavior. You must work to ferret out the competition, jealousy, and any unkindness—and it *is* work! We used all sorts of tactics with a couple of our children: we made them write out and verbally affirm lists of what they admired in one another, we gave them special teamwork assignments to complete together, and I even made them cook meals together for the whole family.

As with other families we are close to, there are certain words which are not permitted in our home. Obvious ones like "stupid," "shut-up," "loser," and "dummy" are forbidden, and are joined by any general attitude of condescension toward or discouraging one another. When I was growing up, there was an unspoken rule that older children did *not* hang out with younger ones. We determined that that exclusion would not happen within our family or our school and church groups. We believe that this *is* "real life"—spending time with those of all different ages, both younger and much older.

We are involved with a high school tutorial that meets once a week to teach upper division college prep classes. The founder, Colleen Whitver, has always stressed the importance of never excluding any student in the classes. During lunch hours or study halls, she could be seen encouraging small "cliques" of students to reach out to any new or unknown kids. This taught my children such consideration and prepared them for college and the workplace.

POP: Gil has always had a heart for serving others—especially his family. I cannot tell you the number of times in the latter years of my dad's life that he would drop everything to go help him—even in the middle of the night! Danielle was every mom's helper at church. She loved babysitting, teaching, and generally planning any fun activities. During college, she helped nanny for several families with whom she is still close. She believes that babysitting includes playing with and cooking for the children, as well as cleaning the house for the family.

Citizen

From an early age, we wanted to instill in our children a sense of patriotism. With the onslaught of revisionist history in our public schools, private schools and homeschoolers will have to continue battling to study the true roots of our Christian founding fathers. We feel an intense obligation to raise up children who are appreciative of the freedoms so dearly won for all of us. We wanted our children to begin early to work to make ours a better community and country. We introduced them to many disciplines that we hoped they would pick up on their own someday. We wrote to soldiers, visited Fort Campbell, and did much campaign work for our area representatives, congressmen, and in the presidential races. We regularly visited nursing homes, did yard work for shut-ins, rehabbed houses, and served at prayer breakfasts for our elected officials. Relevance and exposure to these good works is important in your children's lives.

POP: Several Thanksgivings ago, our three older children were in various life stages: two were in college and one was full-swing into her high school schedule. With such heavy academic loads, the three loved having any time off from school and work obligations. With absolutely no prompting from us, I learned that the three got up early on Thanksgiving morning to serve breakfast to the homeless in downtown Nashville.

Loves learning

I *love* literature and languages. Math and science were "developed" interests for me. My children see me constantly reading and learning because of my belief that learning is a life-long process. I am currently enrolled in a local university completing some graduate work (*very* part-time) for a counseling degree. (I come by this honestly—my mom started her doctorate work at age 67!)

Because I was passionate about literature and language arts, my children seemed to excel more in those areas also. When our oldest was 15 or 16, he began to pray about a perceived calling as a doctor. I have to admit that I experienced some fear about this—not only for his potential years of impossibly hard work, but also in knowing that his strengths were in literature and that medical school exams would be more math- and science-based. I could just see him flunking his MCATS due to my predilection for all things literary!

POP: Will chose a university for its outstanding undergraduate pre-med program. When the professors on the pre-med board called him in to give him the results of his MCAT entrance exam, they said, "Will, you did exceedingly well on the verbal part of the exam." (Now, I could have told them that!) However, the next part gave me such relief: "Med schools now are seeking out applicants who can write well and who can communicate well. Congratulations!" He went on to exceed all their aspirations and is now an anesthesiologist at Vanderbilt Hospital. And he still loves learning!

I love telling this true incident for many reasons. Because we homeschool parents worry so much about shortchanging our children, it is important to realize that we are *not* in control. Understand that God gave you the children He had for you—and that He has called you and prepared you. He *knew* what He had prepared in advance for Will to do—and He knew I would be part of the process to get him there. He will use all your strengths *and* your weaknesses to shape your children. Continue praying for His insight for all your children, and be ready to obey no matter what.

I like this quote by Dorothy Sayers: "Is not the great defect of our education today that although we often succeed in teaching our pupils 'subjects', we fail lamentably on the whole in teaching them how to think: they learn everything, except the art of learning." Learning *is* fun, and it is our primary goal to make as much of their learning as much fun as possible.

Has a heart to serve Jesus

This is definitely our utmost goal in raising our children. God is not limited by our inexperience as parents. He loves taking offered lives and using them for His glory! Everything we did in our homeschool was evaluated on whether it would glorify His name. We wanted them to know Him and desire to serve Him. The Lord has been faithful to call each one of our children into His service in so many different ways.

POP: Believe it or not, we were not very excited about Christian summer camps. We seemed to see much peer pressure and early boyfriend–girlfriend pairings. So our kids never went to any camp except Boy Scout camp, where Tim was always there. This could explain our kids' early interest in summer mission trips! Our kids have worked and lived in Mexico, Honduras, and France—we even allowed our 15-year-old to live near Marseilles for six weeks with a Christian university mission group. Each child had to raise his or her own support for each trip—and came up with many inventive, fun ways to fund-raise. Another self-initiated ministry that our children did was to serve free cold drinks at a large area music festival—all in the name of Jesus. The point is that you can trust God to give such creative ideas to each of your children, using their specific talents and personalities to serve Him.

As you decide on your goals, you may use this list and certainly add to it as you feel the Lord is leading you. You will need to evaluate your husband's participation, the number and ages of your children, your family priorities, your time constraints, and your family's personalities.

As you pray, God will show you what you need to do. Isaiah 48:17 says: "I am the Lord your God—I will show you the way you are to go." You can learn to truly trust that He is in control of your children's education. The following parable illustrates our need to trust so well:

A distinguished group of botanists were high in the Swiss Alps searching for a reported rare specimen of flower. One of them spotted such a sample, but the flower was located on a ledge extending over an immense gorge and could only be reached by someone on a lifeline. These men were in no shape to perform such a daring task at the end of a rope, so they summoned a local village boy. They offered him several gold coins, which he desperately needed. However, he saw the precipice and drew back in fear. He could see no safe way to climb below unless he placed his life in the hands of these strangers. Suddenly, he ran back to the village and returned in a few minutes with a much older man. His solution? He said, "*Now* you may tie the rope on me, and I will descend as long as you let my FATHER hold the rope."

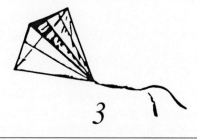

3

Read

"Education has produced a vast population able to read but unable to distinguish what is worth reading."

—G.M.Trevelyan

If you were to ask my grown children today what they enjoyed most about our homeschooling time together, they would all say the book series we read aloud together. There is *nothing* more important you can do for your children's education. I am a firm believer that the book series should be read aloud together, as well as individually. The series will have the impact of involving your family to experience adventures *together*. Our entire family went to the movie premieres of the *Narnia* and *Lord of the Rings* stories, because those were our friends. We met them together—went through their daring adventures, triumphs, and losses together—and we cried together when their time with us was over.

I read books aloud to them from before they could read until they graduated from high school! When I tell people this, they say, "But surely they were reading on their own then!" Of course they were, but there is nothing to compare with hearing for the first time wonderful, living books. And all of your children, no matter what age, will enjoy them *on their own level.*

LeDonna, a homeschooling mom of five, said to me:

> We've read a number of books out loud (following *your* price-
> less advice, my friend!). Among our favorites were *The Hob-
> bit,* the *Lord of the Rings* series, and the complete *Chronicles
> of Narnia.*
> You've made several piercing statements to me over the years.
> (One never knows how what comes out of the mouth or heart
> will impact another!) I am still amazed at what truth they carry.
> One of the statements I was most shocked by was when you
> advocated reading out loud to my teenaged children! After all,
> they could read for themselves, I thought! Why should I do it?
> But I finally relented. Reading aloud became a precious and an-
> ticipated part of our homeschool day. They have *loved* our read-
> aloud times—getting snuggly and excited in a way that children
> of their ages seldom do anymore. I THANK you for that gift,
> my friend. And it is something we must prod the young moth-
> ers coming up behind us to do as well. Some of our most trea-
> sured memories were forged during these pockets of stolen time
> which I originally didn't think I could afford to give.

When asked for her favorite read-alouds, Ginger, a mom of three from Tennessee, says:

> Oh, mercy. Of course *Little House* at least three times all the
> way through. *Chronicles of Narnia,* again too many times
> through to remember. We read the *Little Britches* series and
> the *Boxcar Children. The Borrowers, The Mitchells* (by Hil-
> da van Stockum), *The Bobbsey Twins,* some books that were
> only a few in a series, such as *Caddie Woodlawn,* and *Magical
> Melons.* We read some Katie Johns books. We read *The Soup*
> books and *Billy and Blaze.* The Lois Lenski *Mr. Small* books.
> We read *The Littles.* We read all of Frances Hodgson Burnett's
> books aloud, even though they are not a series. We read all of
> Gene Stratton Porter's books aloud. We read *The Hawk and the
> Dove* aloud. But the absolute BEST, the books my children and
> I loved to read aloud more than any others, were the *Swallows
> and Amazons* by Arthur Ransome. We were totally captivated
> by those books! There are twelve in the series, and they were
> extremely hard to come by. I read them aloud *at least* three

times through. They were wonderful. All three kids would go outside in the afternoons and "play" being the Swallows and Amazons. We still speak in S & A language and have our own funny little family sayings taken from those books.

History comes alive as you read biographies aloud. Dig deep into your library bookshelves, beneath the ridiculous "diverse, multi-cultural, and politically correct" tomes, to get acquainted with the hearts and souls of the God-fearing men who founded our country. Read aloud about those who struggled to press on for freedom, rights, invention, and discovery. You will eventually compile your favorite list as you read together. Some moms have recommended these series:

John Leeper's *Riddle of the Outlaw Bear* and *The Brothers of the Sled*
Scot Penson's *Knights of Evermore*
Meindert DeJong's *The Wheel on the School*
Boxcar Children series
American Girl historical fiction

A mom of two highly successful college graduates says, "We read *Redwall, Watership Down, Blaze, Mother Goose Rhymes, The Children's Homer, All Creatures Great and Small, Tales from Shakespeare,* and the *Oxford Book of Children's Verse,* and books by P.G. Wodehouse were books we read when they were old enough to choose. We read aloud as a family through hundreds of volumes of children's stories when they were very small. Having unlimited time to read aloud together as a family was one of the best rewards of homeschooling."

Back in the early 1980s, we were privileged to hear Dr. Raymond Moore, who is recognized as the first proponent of modern-day home education. He and his wife, Dorothy, have blessed countless families with their godly wisdom and counsel. Dr. Moore advocates reading aloud as one of the greatest char-

acter building exercises possible. He says, "We found construc-
tive *true* stories to be more effective in building character than
myths and novels, because they help to influence the children's
actions and thus their habits, rather than simply amuse."

I certainly read aloud hundreds of single books, and I have a
schoolroom-full to prove it. There is nothing wrong with single
books, which I consider on the same level as memorizing one
Bible verse. That is good, but what is better is memorizing the
entire passage or chapter.

I am frequently asked for my favorite books. Not only do I
have a list of favorite series to read aloud to your children, but I
also have some books that I recommend for homeschool parents
to read for themselves. I have personally met many of the au-
thors of the "mom must-reads" and know that they live out what
they write. Following are some books that I recommend.

Reading List for You:

> *The Ultimate Guide to Homeschooling*—Deborah Bell
> *Dumbing Us Down*—John Taylor Gatto
> *Schoolproof*—Mary Pride
> *For the Children's Sake*—Susan Shaeffer Macaulay
> *The Whole Hearted Child*—Clay & Sally Clarkson
> *Better Late than Early*—Dr. Raymond Moore
> *The Seven Laws of the Learner*—Dr. Bruce Wilkinson
> *How Should We Then Live*—Francis Schaeffer

Read-Aloud Series for Children:

> *The Chronicles of Narnia* series—C.S. Lewis
> The Space Trilogy (older)
> *Little Britches*— Ralph Moody
> Mitford series— Jan Karon
> Missionary series— Patricia St. John

Anne of Green Gables— Lucy Maude Montgomery
Historical Fiction— G.A. Henty
Jungle Missionary series— Ron Snell
Little House series— Laura Ingalls Wilder
Lord of the Rings—J.R.R. Tolkien
Jerusalem Historical Fiction (older)—Brock & Bodie Thoene
Little Women—Louisa May Alcott
The Borrowers—Mary Norton
Tom Sawyer and *The Adventures of Huckleberry Finn*—
    Mark Twain
First-Century Historical Fiction— Lloyd C. Douglas
Jeeves: Dry British humor (older)— P.G. Wodehouse

An additional tip to help the learning process during read-alouds is to allow your children to constructively "doodle." This means employing creative methods to engage their brain while you are reading out loud. Over the years, I have used many teaching strategies to help this process. Here are some examples:

- While reading the *Lord of the Rings*, I had them each draw their rendition of what Gandalf looked like (this was long before the movie interpretation!).
- While reading aloud some of the Henty historical fiction books, I had them design our own family coat of arms.
- There are a number of great detailed coloring books (my favorites are Dover and Ravensburger). Many have intricate stained-glass designs, puzzle-within-a-picture drawings, and architectural designs to color.
- Make sure that there is NO reading on the paper, for that will distract from your read-aloud. I certainly let my younger ones and my kinesthetic learners (they have to have *something* to fidget with!) play with Lincoln Logs, Legos, Coinstruction, and other hands-on manipulatives. This really does propel the learning process as they listen.
- And last, but not least, I have definitely resorted to having

them all fold clothes and mate socks. If we are going to succeed at this home education endeavor, it is going to take all
of us working together!

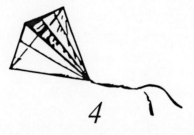

4

Memorize

"The object of teaching a child is to enable him to get along without a teacher."

—Elbert Hubbard

As you begin this journey of homeschooling, you will realize that your children learn in different ways. God did this to test you—to see if *you* could learn! Seriously, too many of us, after our first-born, think every other child will be a strong-willed visual learner. Then we have our next one!

God has gifted each one of our children—THEY'RE ALL GIFTED! It is truly a marvelous privilege to watch them as they grow and respond, and to tailor their learning experiences to the way they are made. There are many methods out there to ascertain how your child learns. One easy way to confirm if your child is, indeed, an auditory learner is to tell them to remember a number in the thousands. You will need to write this number down because *you* will forget it. Ask them the number the next day, and then the next, and then in three weeks. If they remember a sufficiently hard number after three weeks, it is pretty likely that they learn in an auditory way.

Following is a quick checklist that you can do with your children. (It may help immensely to find out what sort of learner *you* are!) Remember that although each child can be a combination learner, he or she learns primarily through one sense.

Learning Styles Checklist
Learner Section 1
- I remember what I read better than what I hear.
- I am able to visualize what pages look like in books I've read.
- Looking at pictures and charts helps me remember facts.
- When I am trying to learn something new, it helps me to form a picture of it in my mind.
- I remember people's faces better than their names.

Learner Section 2
- I prefer to listen to the teacher instead of reading new material.
- I understand things better when I discuss them with others.
- I can usually remember what I hear.
- I understand material best when I read it aloud.
- I talk to myself when I try to solve problems.

Learner Section 3
- I study best when I can move around.
- I take notes in order to understand the material.
- I move my lips when I read and use my fingers to count.
- I learn best when I can handle objects.
- I would rather just get started instead of reading or listening to directions.

1: Visual learner – needs to see something written down to remember it best
2: Auditory learner – needs to hear or discuss material
3: Kinesthetic/Tactile learner – needs to personally experience things

Upon learning which style best fits your child, you are then ready to tailor some of your curricula to that particular style. I read everything aloud to my auditory learner—certainly into high school! His strength was that he could remember almost everything he heard. This helped him immensely later in his college lecture classes. We were able to find many books on tape (such a God-send for us!). His problem was that it would take him so long to read something, that by the time he got to the end of the thought, he had forgotten the first part. It was necessary for us to play to his strength of listening.

Memorization is a daily strategy to lead your children to academic success. The choices you make for your children to memorize will depend solely on your interests, their callings, and your available talents and time. Repetition together as a family early in the school day is key. When my daughter was three years old, she loved saying the Pledge of Allegiance because she heard her older brothers say it faithfully every morning! Make a game or contest of memorizing, and present it as a program to their dad at night, to grandparents on holidays, or to nursing home residents anytime. Some suggested memorization from homeschool moms across the country include:

Pledge of Allegiance
Preamble to the Constitution
Poetry (for example, Poe's *"The Raven," "Charge of the Light Brigade," "Casey at the Bat," "High Flight,"* or any of Wordsworth)
Phonics rules from *The Writing Road to Reading*
Multiplication Tables
Gettysburg Address
The American's Creed
World history dates from Hillyer's *A Child's History of the World*
The One Hundred Root Words from *English from the Roots Up*

Susan, a homeschooling mom of seven, has had her children memorize many chapters in the New Testament. She includes the Sermon on the Mount (Matthew 5–7), Romans 8 and 12, I Corinthians 13, and Hebrews 11 and 12.

A homeschooling mom of six loved to use songs to enhance memorization. She remembers using songs to help her children memorize the names of planets, the states, and even their phone number. One of her favorite Psalms is: "Because You are my help, I sing in the shadow of Your wings. My soul clings to You; Your right hand upholds me." Knowing this gifted mom (and worship leader) makes me appreciate how much she depends on the Lord's help.

Another mom from Georgia advocates memorizing "math facts, spelling rules, vocabulary, geography (states and capitals as well as countries and capitals), and Bible songs."

Many homeschoolers employ songs in memorization. There are many excellent tapes available using geography, math facts, and Bible verses. I encourage you to allow your children to listen to Bible tapes as they fall asleep.

Memorizing Bible passages is rather straight-forward. A good way to involve both your visual and auditory learners is to take poster board, write out your intended passage, and then repeat out loud together one line at a time. Even the youngest child can join in this exercise. Many times, I reward a prize at the end of a particularly long passage. Then, when a passage has been memorized, I allow them to decorate the margin of the poster board during read-alouds. We then display our poster in our school room. What a great reminder of God's living word!

The Lord will be faithful to show you passages that will bless you and each child. If you think back to your own Sunday school days, I bet you will remember chapters you memorized. Please remember that "*all* Scripture is God-breathed and is useful for teaching, rebuking, correcting and training in righteousness so that the man of God may be thoroughly equipped for every good work" (II Timothy 3:16, emphasis mine). As a help to you, I have listed some of our favorites.

Psalm 1	John 1:1–14
Psalm 23	John 14:1–21
Psalm 100	Romans 8
Psalm 27:1–5	Romans 12
Psalm 63	I Corinthians 13
Psalm 91	Ephesians 1
Proverbs 1:1–8	Ephesians 4:1–16
Proverbs 3	Ephesians 6:1–18
Proverbs 16:1–9	Philippians 1:1–9
Proverbs 31	Philippians 2:1–16
Ecclesiastes 3:1–8	Philippians 4:4–9
Isaiah 6:1–8	Colossians 1:9–20
Isaiah 9:2–7	Colossians 3:12–25
Isaiah 53	Hebrews 11
Isaiah 61	Hebrews 12:1–11
Matthew 5	II Peter 1:3–7

Our children never outgrow the need to memorize. You are imparting a life lesson that will serve them well always. One of my grown children heard the following declaration read in church and was so moved by the affirmations that he wanted to memorize it.

> Today I am stepping across the line. I am tired of waffling and I am finished with wavering; I've made my choice, the verdict is in, and my decision is irrevocable. I'm going God's way. There is no turning back now!
>
> I will live the rest of my life serving God's purposes with God's people on God's planet for God's glory. I will use my life to celebrate His presence, cultivate His character, participate in His family, demonstrate His love, and communicate His word.
>
> Since my past has been forgiven and I have a purpose for living and a home awaiting in heaven, I refuse to waste any more time or energy on shallow living, petty thinking, trivial talking, thoughtless doing, useless regretting, hurtful resent-

ing, or faithless worrying. Instead, I will magnify God, grow to maturity, serve in ministry, and fulfill my mission in the membership of His family.

Because this life is preparation for the next, I will value worship over wealth, "we" over "me," character over comfort, service over status, and people over possessions, position, and pleasures. I know what matters most and I'll give it all I've got. I'll do the best I can with what I have for Jesus Christ today.

I won't be captivated by culture, manipulated by critics, motivated by praise, frustrated by problems, debilitated by temptation, or intimidated by the devil. I'll keep running my race with my eyes on the goal, not the sidelines or those running by me. When things get tough, and I get tired, I won't back up, back off, back down, back out, or backslide. I'll just keep moving forward by God's grace. I'm Spirit-led, purpose-driven, and mission-focused, so I cannot be bought, I will not be compromised, and I shall not quit until I finish the race.

I'm a trophy of God's amazing grace, so I will be gracious to everyone, grateful for everyday, and generous with everything that God entrusts to me. To my Lord Jesus I say:

"However, whenever, wherever, and whatever you ask me to do, my answer in advance is yes! Wherever you lead and whatever the cost, I'm ready. Anytime. Anywhere. Anyway. Whatever it takes Lord! I want to be used by you in such a way, that on that final day I'll hear you say, 'Well done, thou good and faithful one. Come on in, and let the eternal party begin!'"

Memorization is such an important strategy and help for your children's future education. Israel slid into idolatry and almost total extinction because the fathers did not teach their children to teach their children. Psalm 78:4–7: "We will tell the next generation the praiseworthy deeds of the Lord, His power and the wonders He has done... so the next generation would know them, even the children yet to be born, and they in turn would tell their children. Then they would put their trust in God and would not forget His deeds but would keep His commands."

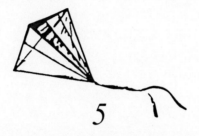

5

Simplify

"That man is richest whose pleasures are the cheapest."
—Henry David Thoreau

Two men cut wood all day long. One worked straight through the day, without stopping to rest. At the end of the day, he had a sizable pile of logs.

The other would chop for fifty minutes and then take a ten minute break. He did this every hour, all day long. At the end of the day he had a much larger pile than the first man. "How could you chop more?" asked the man who worked continuously. His friend replied, "Every time I stopped to rest, I also sharpened my axe!"

Proverbs 27:17— "As iron sharpens iron, so one man sharpens another."

We homeschoolers tend to become hampered with *too much*, and then beat ourselves up for not being able to accomplish all of it. One of the most liberating life lessons I can share with you is that *you will skip things*! I'm serious—you will skip *multitudes* of things! We all do—there is no getting around that fact. I would never advocate laziness or apathy, but every teacher leaves out masses of information. Think back to your own schooling. How many textbooks did you actually finish? I thought so.

The key, after praying, planning, and creating, is to *simplify.* This means simplify your goals, your schedule, your school-room, your house, and your thoughts. This is an ongoing process, but you can start here with a simple checklist that I call "The Plate Spinner." I think homeschool moms wrote the book on how many different plates are able to be kept aloft, spinning all the while! I actually use this list in my own life once a year, and it has given me needed sanity when I pare down my life to live simply. I have included this as one complete list for you to copy and put on your refrigerator. Following this list is an explanation of each section.

"The Plate Spinner"

Ask yourself these questions regarding CLUTTER:
    1. Will this be useful in the near future?
    2. Have I used this in the past year?
    3. Do I have too many of this?
    4. Is this in the way more than it is used?
    5. Could someone else use this more than our family?

Ask yourself these questions regarding EXTRA-CURRICU-LAR ACTIVITIES:
    1. What is our motivation?
    2. Is this preparing my child for a career or lifestyle consistent with our convictions?
    3. Are our children old enough that the good outweighs the potential harm?
    4. How will this affect our family time?

Ask yourself these questions regarding TEACHING:
1. Am I making the simple difficult?
2. Do I need to be doing this at all?
3. What are my long- and short-term goals?
4. Should I give this a rest?

Ask yourself these questions regarding your ENERGY LEVEL:
1. Am I eating a balanced diet?
2. Am I receiving adequate sleep for my season of life?
3. Am I making time for aerobic exercise?
4. Am I acknowledging sufficient rewards for my efforts?
5. Am I able to relax in spite of circumstances?
6. Am I obeying the biblical mandate to rejoice?

With the vast accumulation of all consumable goods, it is vital for homeschoolers to regularly de-clutter. Studies have proven that chaotic physical clutter can have a devastating effect on our spiritual and mental well-being. Because we work at home, learn at home, experiment and create at home, we need to be vigilant in keeping our homes relatively clutter-free. I used the term "relatively" because we will always have learning resources at hand in our home laboratory. But the periphery of our lives can be simplified. Although each mom can certainly recognize what she calls clutter, my list would include clothing, knick-knacks, kitchen paraphernalia, toiletries, games, magazines, and décor. You need to ask these practical questions once a year and *act on them*.

Ask yourself these questions regarding CLUTTER:

Will this be useful in the near future?
An embarrassing example of mine used to be the magazine racks full of old Reader's Digests. While we all love them when they first come in the mail, I had to ask myself, *why* am I saving them? Do I really believe my life will slow down enough that I will go back after all those years and re-read them? Besides, if I

desire to look up a specific past article, I can bring it up online.
Call your local nursing home to see if they would like a dona-
tion, and if not...straight to the recycling bin. As far as other
magazines go, I have a file system for articles I want to save,
with folders such as decorating and travel ideas, "Mighty Men,"
and marriage articles.

Another way to apply this question is when evaluating clothes,
whether yours or your children's. For example, if your last baby
is now twelve, chances are your maternity clothes are incredibly
old and out-of-style. Get rid of them! If you do get pregnant again
(I did after thirteen years), there are consignment stores, thrift
shops, and excited gift-giving friends! Get rid of it.

Have I used this in the past year?

Dehydrators, food processors, space/air vacuums, bread ma-
chines, and other time-saving gadgets seem helpful at the time,
but can really be a weight we don't need. Can you borrow one
of these implements when the time comes (if it ever does)? Besides taking up space, what usually happens to me is that I feel
guilty for not using them—and we deal with enough guilt already! Give your rarely used items to a sister-in-law or friend
who doesn't homeschool, and then just borrow it if you need it.
Get rid of it.

Do I have too many of this?

This possibly seems a weird question *until* you start evaluating your household. In my own case, I had a friend whose gift
was organization, and she came over several afternoons to help
me start the process. Imagine my surprise, when cleaning out
an especially deep cupboard drawer, at finding almost thirty
potholders! You should know that I have never bought a single
potholder. These were wedding presents, gifts from friends when
I remodeled our kitchen several times, and unreturned ones left
by friends who came for meals! Now that I've gotten rid of most
of them, I have another great storage drawer for large items. You

would be amazed at the freedom you feel when you purge un-wanted and unneeded items!

Also be sure to check your make-up and toiletries. Seri-ously, how many samples of lotion do you need? If you feel badly throwing them away, make a zip lock bag and donate it to a women's shelter. Get rid of it.

Is this in the way more than it is used?

Here in Western abundance, we tend to accumulate. In order to have a clean, clutter-free environment to best teach our chil-dren and enjoy our family, we have to continually go against the culture. Look around at all the knick-knacks that you have col-lected over the years—are they necessary? Or does it drain your time dusting them (or drain your energy with guilt of *not* having dusted them)? If you are constantly moving things in order to get on with your teaching day, please re-consider if you need them at all. Get rid of it.

Could someone else use this more than our family?

Simplicity is freedom. If you camp, think about the things you pack for a weekend trip. Except for food, what else do you really need to live? Simplify your environment. Look around to see if you can bless someone less fortunate with some of your "extras." Quit going to the "big-box" stores only to have to ar-range for storage for huge vats of mayonnaise, bulk vitamins, and garages full of toilet paper.

Be reasonable—shop with coupons to get the price breaks, and quit housing unnecessary consumable goods. Get rid of them. We have given away cars, canned goods, lots of furniture, pets, and of course, clothes. There can be such a blessing to those receiving. You never know when you may be hearing a nudge from God to answer someone else's needs.

Do you see a recurring theme? You will feel a hundred pounds lighter as you de-clutter and change from a shopping/gathering mentality to a creating/enjoying lifestyle.

Unlike when we began homeschooling, today there are myriads of options for extra-curricular activities. Everything from chess clubs and drama troupes to all types of sports and debate teams is available—*for a price.* I am not speaking of your money, but your *time.* For each good thing you choose for your child, you give up your time, your child's time, and your family's time. Scheduling should serve us—not the other way around. Scheduling our time wisely will create the balance God intends. God will give you discernment on balancing your schedule if you slow down long enough to ask for His guidance and listen to Him!

We recommend asking these questions when considering each activity that you commit your family to. I use the word "commit" on purpose. I believe in elementary grades that you should expose your children to as many subjects as possible (breadth) to discern interest and ability. (The depth in these specific areas should come later in upper high school.) However, the groups and teams you want to involve your child in will most likely require a commitment. This is only fair to the coach or teacher. So, pray diligently, evaluate carefully, and proceed cautiously.

Ask yourself these questions regarding EXTRA-CURRICULAR ACTIVITIES:

What is our motivation?
Some of us were high school athletes and remember it as a time of discipline, teamwork, and excitement. We too often forget the unhurried, unscheduled, and un-coached carefree days of playing football or baseball in our backyards. We cannot recreate those days, but we should not embrace the mindset that we have to jump into supervised, costly, segregated teams when our children are very young. Examine why you want to pursue any team, and evaluate whether exposure to these potential elements, which sadly could include verbally abusive coaches and parents,

exclusivist mentality, and acute comparison, is beneficial at this particular age.

Lately, we have seen an amazing increase of homeschoolers in competitive sports. This overall tendency is positive, yet a disturbing trend has been the mindset of competing for college scholarships at all costs. While a tiny, select number of student athletes nationwide have been granted monetary aid for college athletics, this is certainly not the norm. The "Tommy Tebow" story made news because it *is* phenomenal—not normal. I want to warn most parents that to believe their children will achieve that status is, at best, incredibly unrealistic. Besides sacrificing irreplaceable family time, service projects, and increased study time, we set up our children for intense disappointment. Travel teams and specialized coaching are robbing families of money, quality church time, and many vacations, not to mention quiet family time at home. "I've never see a Kentucky Derby won by a mule" is a saying from a college coach that explains the fact that even with hard work, God gives limits to how far we can go athletically. It is a disservice to your children if they are insulated to the point where they are 5'10" and still dreaming of playing power forward in college. The Lord points us to balance in all things, and harried moms driving from practice to practice need to remember that. Please don't subject your family to a schedule which is punishing and fruitless, all for the sake of unrealistic goals. Our family loves sports and the teamwork mentality it entails. We would not trade the lessons learned or the relationships gained from all our many years on sports teams. I am specifically addressing the families who pursue sports above all else. You will regret later the misplaced priorities.

Is this preparing my child for a career or lifestyle consistent with our convictions?

I have asked this question to parents who enroll young children in classes such as jazz dance. This activity could eventually culminate in skimpy costumes, questionable music, and inappropriate movements. What seems innocent and "precious" at a young age needs to be followed to its logical outcome.

The same question should be asked of those teams—sports, debate, and others—which would cause much missed church attendance and fellowship as your children progress.

Are our children old enough that the good outweighs the potential harm?

You can control your children's environment for such a short time. As they mature and are more ready for outside competitive situations, only you can determine how much is too much. Realize that your children will encounter insensitivity, injustice, and rejection, whether it's in sports, music, or other activities. From my experience, and others I've talked to, the best age to begin a musical instrument is second grade. Organized sports teams tend to recruit much earlier, and it is up to you to guard and protect your children's spirits until you feel they are ready.

How will this affect our family time?

I have previously addressed the time issue that most teams require. Another factor to consider is how all the other non-participating family members feel about the output of time necessary for each extra-curricular endeavor. Some families will not understand the cumulative resentment felt by these other children until years later. Is it fair to drag the younger siblings and have them spend untold hours doing nothing but waiting on their big brother to finish a practice or tournament? Evaluate how many meals you are eating in the car and at the ballpark or gym. The expense alone for these ready-made meals must be factored into the cost of each activity (a cost which already includes uniforms, refs, gym rental, etc.). Sit down with each family member and honestly assess how these activities will affect them.

As more children in your family come of the age to be involved in sports and other activities, realistically look at your calendar. Do you need to set a boundary to limit one sport per season? Some of you reading this might find that proposal ridiculous, but in our neighborhoods, there is increased pressure to make soccer, baseball, and basketball year-round sports. You can imagine what happens when the basketball tournaments overlap into the baseball season. Seriously—stop the madness. Pare down. Enjoy a sport at a time, without the unnecessary added stress of believing it will lead to a college scholarship.

Ask yourself these questions regarding TEACHING:

Am I making the simple difficult?

When I am teaching a unit for our homeschool group that meets one afternoon a week for history and science projects, I frequently use the internet for ideas. I am absolutely amazed (and appalled) at the educational psycho-babble posted there intended to introduce teachers to the objectives they need to reach. Someone needs to brand that as hogwash! Our school system seems to major in ways to make the simple difficult. We, as consumers of curricula designed to be in a school setting, should beware of "educationese." Each curricula publisher has one goal: to sell curricula. If they can prey on our fear of "not doing enough," it will guarantee more profit for them. We need to impart true, relevant learning at a pace which coincides with our children's abilities, and in a manner which correlates to their learning styles.

Many school systems reject the teaching of phonics and later never wonder why their students' spelling is horrific and their reading comprehension below grade level. Phonics is an essential start, but expensive bells and whistles in the program are not necessary. Consistently read aloud and expose your children to great, living literature. Periodically evaluate their reading comprehension by verbally asking them to narrate back what they've heard. Chart their successes on spelling tests and watch their vocabulary increase. Re-evaluate your phonics and spelling program each year for each child. This sounds tedious, but it is vital to understanding how each child best learns. There are so many different curricula publishers competing for your money, and they will attempt to convince you that your child's education will be lacking without their "new" product. Pray for discernment, and never buy the entire grade level of any publisher. As your confidence and expertise in each child's learning style increases, you will make wiser choices—and you will certainly learn from your own mistakes!

Do I need to be doing this at all?

Sometimes, in our "relentless pursuit of perfection," we think that each child must complete each textbook, each workbook page, and each line of our particular scope and sequence. I personally have perused two such scope and sequences: those published by World Book Encyclopedia and A Beka. While these can be a legitimate help, they never need to propel us into unneeded frustration. Although it is necessary to prepare, only God knows the future He has prepared in advance for our children. I have found, in hindsight, that the topics I was most worried about skipping were practically unnecessary for that particular child.

We never specifically studied map skills in elementary school, yet all my children performed credibly on the achievement tests. I remember one hectic year in which one of my children never had any science (outside of a few group experiments)—and yet his score improved on the yearly standardized test. I used Saxon Math from fourth grade through the Calculus books, and never used Saxon 87 (which is a sequential math study used in eighth grade). While using Saxon, I never once had my children do all thirty problems per lesson—we always did either the even or odd numbers. Remember, this was written for a classroom of *thirty*—you *know* the concepts that your student has attained and the ones he or she has yet to master.

I will never advocate cutting corners or being lazy or shortchanging our children in their educational walk. But you must be prayerful *and* use common sense *and* obtain godly counsel on what to teach your children. This truly is my motivation for writing this book: to help encourage wise use of your time and resources, alleviate worry and stress for unnecessary work, and add *joy* to your home!

"Sometimes our activity, our work, is nothing more than a cheap imitation to deaden the pain of an empty life." In our western world of materialistic abandon, we recognize this as truth, but what makes this quote especially ironic is that it was written by Adolf Coors IV. Obviously, the name Coors is synonymous with beer—which to excess is "a cheap imitation to deaden the pain of an empty life." We must never engage our students in meaningless or empty work but strive to engage them in relevant, purposeful activity.

Don't Miss The Dolphins!

On our latest trip to Destin, Florida, we were walking the beach as usual. We love going to Destin for several reasons, besides it being the closest beach to our home in Nashville. The sand is always pure white and the water is crystal blue-green. On this particular trip, Luke had found three amazing shells, and Danielle and I were "power-walking" while Luke scoured every strand before running to catch up with us. We were all so intent on discovering what new "treasure" God was going to reveal to us that we almost completely missed one of His best! An older couple grabbed our attention and told us to stop and look at two dolphins playing quite close to the shore! They told us that they had been in Destin for two months and looked every day for dolphins but this was the first time they had seen them!

I think all of us get too involved in the search for "treasures." I do not mean the all-too-common pursuit of money. I'm speaking of how we pursue making a difference—how we each see our own importance—and that sometimes, by keeping our focus on the next big thing, we miss what God really wants to show us.

We can miss the dolphins, never knowing they were even there at all!

An even better example occurred a few years ago. On our land in the country, we seem to always have a variety of animals. Since we live close to a highway, we have lost many pets due to car traffic. When our adopted grandfather, Dock, lived with us, he shared such an attachment to them—especially the dogs. We all hated losing pets, but Dock seemed most affected.

On one hot August morning, we were filled with dread upon hearing screeching brakes. Dock actually made it down the driveway first, followed by Tim and one of his employees. I watched sadly from the house as they loaded an animal's body in the back of our truck. I was puzzled, however, as I watched the three of them continue to search along the sides of the road. It was a sweltering day, and I couldn't imagine what they were possibly looking for.

I learned the rest of the story later that day. It seems that Dock and Tim had found the body of a pet dog (which was not ours, but a neighbor's). The rather gruesome discovery was that the vehicle that had hit him had apparently severed his front leg. The men hated the thought of telling our neighbor the bad news, but could not stand taking the mangled body back without the leg—thus the search on the hot highway.

After a fruitless hour, Tim and his co-worker prepared to go inform our neighbor of the tragedy. The grandmother answered the door. Tim decided to keep his voice low in order to not upset the little girl who lived there. However, upon hearing the bad news, the grandmother loudly exclaimed, "Oh NO! Maddie's DEAD!" Of course, her screams brought the ten-year-old girl to the door as Tim tried to be as quiet and sensitive as possible. The grandmother continued wailing: "Oh, what are we going to do? Maddie's dead—how are we going to tell Michael [her son]? Especially after he just spent so much money having her leg *amputated*!"

The men had spent much time searching for something that

was *not there in the first place*! I love this true story, for it illustrates a practical principle: we should never get "bent out of shape" attempting to force what was *not* intended. God has specific plans for each of our children, and we should be discerning enough to walk in His leading for them. We should not force our imperfect vision on them; otherwise, we may be looking for the missing leg on a three-legged dog!

What are my long- and short-term goals?

Mastery learning is the homeschooler's secret weapon. We are *not* bound by worksheets, or texts being completed on artificial timetables. We should always teach until we *know* that our children know and understand—and then *stop*. There is always reason to remind and update, but we never have to continue to work problem after problem to know that they understand a concept.

Write down your goals. They will change as you accomplish more, but you need a written target and a record for evaluation. Decide what *is* worth your expended effort for this phase in your children's lives.

Should I give this a rest?

The following true story has already given hope to countless families who have heard me speak. We all know (either from our own school experience or any scope and sequence) that a student must learn multiplication in the third grade. Some advanced math programs introduce the concept in second grade, but third grade is the definite benchmark.

I knew our firstborn was highly intelligent—not only from personal observation, but also from confirmation of test scores. So, when we were beginning multiplication in the fall of third grade, I had no qualms at all with his ability to handle it. However, he had a *major* stumbling block, and was just not able to understand it. I felt unbelievable pressure to *make* him understand for a couple of reasons: 1) of course, every child must learn multiplication in the third grade! And 2) we were under a microscope as far as our families were concerned about this whole new radical concept of teaching your children at home. Subsequently, I put enormous pressure on him—and it was truly a stressful, unproductive time. When we were both in tears, I stopped and thought, *Is this really what teaching should be?*

Thankfully I felt convicted to stop the madness—and just forget math for a while. When that stress was removed, Will relaxed and flourished in all the other subjects we were studying at the time. I simply prayed (and worried), but did not attempt to do any more math for several months. In that period, God led me to a godly older homeschooler who asked me if I had ever heard of Cuisinaire rods. I had not, and immediately headed to a teaching aid store and bought them.

On the first day of classes after Christmas, I told Will that I had found a game that I thought would make math more fun. We worked with the rods for a few minutes and then I saw the light bulb go off in his head—it was amazing! He said, "I get it! Can we do this all day?" Of course, since we were homeschooling, I was able to say, "Yes, we *can* do multiplication all day!"

In any other school situation, there would have been a schedule—an artificial timetable—to follow, and the only thing Will would have learned that fall would have been to hate math. And, if by some unlikely chance a wise teacher had stopped and waited for the right timing, there is still no way that upon mastering it, he could have had the freedom to "play" all day with the newly acquired concept.

Timing is key to learning—especially with boys. It has always been a mystery to me to hear the experts state that boys lag behind girls on all levels of maturity in the lower grades, and yet they expect girls *and* boys to learn to read in the first grade. Is there any wonder that so many more boys "act out," are labeled ADD, and are actually miserable in the structured, inflexible seatwork world of the classroom?

Ask yourself these questions regarding your ENERGY LEVEL:

Am I eating a balanced diet?

This question can be more adequately answered by those much more knowledgeable than I. Realize that your health will be partially determined by your diet—and that you will experience mood swings, lethargy, and artificial hyperactivity if you are remiss in monitoring your meals.

Am I receiving adequate sleep for my season of life?

Obviously, at any given point in a mom's life, there can be many reasons for lack of sleep. Pregnancy, nursing, remodeling, and having a 16-year-old driver all come to mind. However, knowing that you must be prepared with a clear focus in your teaching has to become a priority.

Your husband must understand that he is your first love, followed by your children. You can help him *help you* by gently asking for some help around the house while your children are too young to be very effective. The two of you can decide together, for a season, what is "the absolute least you can live with" (as far as housekeeping). As your older ones assume responsibility for more duties, this will enable you to relax more and enjoy time with your husband.

Am I making time for aerobic exercise?

I cannot emphasize enough the need for some sort of aerobic exercise incorporated into your week. I believe the minimum for effective stress relief is three half-hour sessions per week. As far as what exercise you choose, be creative! Some moms love their early-morning treadmill time before the household is awake. Other "night owls" prefer catching up on late night TV while "spinning." Some families love to bike together on weekends, with the mom getting in a couple of tours during the week. Or the whole family might take up hiking and backpacking, and turn trails into field trips.

I joined a Christian aerobic/dance class to shed pounds after my first three children and loved it so much that I became an instructor, and later the owner of the company! Even though my schedule sometimes required me to teach a morning class, my children were young enough then that I could place them in a nearby Sunday school classroom with seatwork to do for an hour until I was finished. And the money I made instructing certainly helped with the cost of curricula! When my children were very young, my schedule could be more flexible as far as schoolwork was concerned. This "outside" time had to be adjusted as my children needed more instructional time. As always, the only workout that will work will be the one that you *do*. Discover what works for your family.

Am I acknowledging sufficient rewards for my efforts?

A definition of *burnout* is receiving inadequate positive feedback for your expended efforts. We will all experience this at times, but homeschool moms are especially vulnerable. For the most part, our children will not appreciate or thank us for our sacrifice until years later.

So, it is up to us to patiently persevere, knowing that we are called by God to raise up this next generation. Dwell in His presence and soak up His approval. He *sees* and *knows* what we do every day. In addition, plan something every day (or at least every week) to which you look forward. For me, this often involves reading a good book—*just for me* (it can have nothing to do with home schooling or Christian growth).

For all you moms reading this, *now* is the time to highlight this next paragraph and leave it in the bathroom for your husband.

Husbands, your wives *must* have a break from their never-ending jobs as homeschool moms. Many evenings you will be tempted to say, "Honey, just sit down right here and relax." You need to know that this is pretty much impossible. She works at home, and no matter where she sits, she can see an unfinished pile of *something*—and it will not let her relax. So, one night a week, you need to take her out somewhere. I'm not suggesting anywhere especially expensive. I know finances can be tough because you are working the equivalent of two jobs so that she is able to stay home and teach the children. Take her on a picnic, to a park, to a bookstore reading room, or to a matinee—but get her out! She needs it and she will be very grateful. Ultimately, you will be too!

Am I able to relax in spite of circumstances?

Each homeschooling family will encounter great stresses and seasons of grief—this is a part of life. I believe it is so important for children to watch us as we undergo these stresses, and learn from our example. I had many mornings when I had to stop everything and ask my kids to pray for my attitude. Sometimes it was just a complaining/self-pitying attitude; other times it was sadness or feelings of being overwhelmed. (I also had sixteen weeks of horrendous morning sickness when our oldest was a senior and we were applying for college scholarships!) The only way we can relax and leave the details to God is if we can believe He is able and if we will release our fears to Him. Circumstances will always change, but He is always the same.

Am I obeying the biblical mandate to rejoice?

Joy does not have to be elusive in our homes. We should not make the mistake of believing we will rejoice when the kids are in college. They must see us with a mindset of joy and contentment. If we are not regularly teaching our children the character trait of gratitude, we should. Our children try to remember to always thank their Sunday school teachers, coaches, and tutors for each session spent with them. Learning to instill gratefulness is a process, as is learning to rejoice in all things.

Anita from Iowa shares this awesome idea for simplifying a handwriting course:

> Combine the exercise of practicing handwriting, Bible memorization, art, and letter writing. Instead of writing silly phrases

over and over, they would choose a verse. They would practice
their handwriting, writing the verse again and again, which
helped them to remember it also. Then four or five days later,
they would write it nicely on a piece of wide-lined paper and
then decorate it with crayons and markers. I would then have
them choose a person to send it to and have them write that
person a short note.

We tend to over-purchase everything from curricula to pencils.
There is truly too much emphasis on textbooks and workbooks.
We need to step back and review what is really important in a
balanced education. From an article entitled the "Frugal Educa-
tor" there were listed these ten essential things which actually
could constitute all you need for your homeschool tools:

1. The Bible
2. The dictionary
3. A library card
4. A phone book
5. A journal
6. Memorization
7. Collections
8. Read-alouds
9. Maps
10. Singing

Stop the rush. Sit down. Laugh. Read. Pray. This is education.

Isn't that refreshing? All of us need to simplify our busy, hectic,
activity-filled lives. This simple list pares down all we think we
need into a real essential tool of learning.

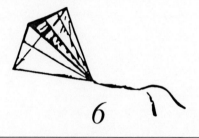

6

$\mathcal{G}row$

"Poor is the pupil who does not surpass his master."
—Leonardo da Vinci

Growth is such a rich, variegated word. The whole lifestyle of home education is the most effective method of intellectual growth, but that is not our total goal. We have the glorious opportunity and time to emotionally protect, to intellectually challenge, and to spiritually disciple those entrusted to us. Wow! What a challenge—with God's help this is attainable.

We encouraged our children to celebrate growth in lifelong learning. Among other things, we used gardening, raising all types of animals, and the entire concept of teams to teach them the hard daily discipline of growth. One such catalyst we used was our family's love of beekeeping. We have harvested honey for years, to all of our extended family's delight. Look around you at your particular circumstances to see how you can use gardens, animals, teams, and local ministries to encourage your children to grow.

When I look at how Jesus grew, one verse stands out to me:

"He grew in wisdom and in stature and in favor with God and man" (Luke 2:52). I believe we can pattern our growth as home-school moms training the next generation of leaders in the same way. Of course, we need the Scriptures to teach us how to grow up our children.

Jesus Grew in Wisdom

Intellectual growth can be a wonderful by-product of our one-on-one tutorial learning. We should strive to be effective disciplers. The effective teacher teaches from an overflow of a full life. I want to be a running stream for my children, and not a stagnant pond!

I need to grow up and accept responsibility for my own intel-lectual growth. What are you spending your time doing? Do you say to yourself, "I just want to check my e-mail"—and look up an hour later, realizing you have wasted that hour! An excellent tip is to set a ten-minute timer every time you go online—and stick to it. Are you watching inane TV? If you can't discipline yourself to limit what you are watching and how much, get rid of it! (Our ten years without a TV were the most productive, creative, fun times ever.) Are you reading impractical magazines? Be discerning in your choices. Choose to read that which enriches your mind. Wean yourself away from distractions, and grow in wisdom!

Jesus Grew in Stature

This is obviously Jesus' physical growth. In the previous chapter I included a checklist that recommended consistent aero-bic exercise. We need that outlet to stay balanced. Exercise helps us not only cope with stress, but it also aids in problem solving, enhances enthusiasm, and multiplies our energy. WE NEED IT! Romans 6 tells us that we need to offer our bodies to God as an instrument of righteousness.

Jesus Grew in Favor with Man

I believe this correlates with our emotional growth. Every

homeschool mom should write the following on a card and put it on her mirror: "You will never get it all _____." The journey of home education is basically an unending, thankless, unfinished, sacrificial process which God will complete in *His* timing. When we truly believe that, we will be set free from needless worry.

I believe we all need an intimate support group of people to encourage us on this awesome, challenging journey. Be willing to be vulnerable and ask for help! Your immediate relations, your church family, and your homeschool support group should all be integral to your work.

Jesus Grew in Favor with God

The more I change, the more I can become an instrument of change in my children's lives. I believe that homeschool moms have the same job description as the Old Testament priests. The priest's job was to represent God to the people and to present the people to God. In a similar way, we represent God to our children and we will present our children to God. As we ask the Lord to grow us up as Jesus grew, we need to grow in accountability, in responsibility, and in life skills.

Grow in Accountability

God will cause much growth in our walk through transparency. There is a story of a mom with multiple children, and on this one particularly hectic day she was having trouble doing even routine chores. Her irritation revolved around her three-year-old son who was on her heels no matter where she went. Whenever she stopped to do something and turned around, she would practically trip over him. Several times she patiently suggested fun activities to keep him occupied. "Wouldn't you like to play on the swing set?" she asked. But he simply smiled an innocent smile and said, "That's okay Mommy; I'd rather be in here with you." Then he continued to bounce happily behind her. After stepping on his toes, she started to lose her patience and insisted that he go outside with the other children. When she asked him why he was acting this way, he looked up at her and said, "Well Mommy, in Sunday school, my teacher told me to walk in Jesus' footsteps. But I cannot see Him, so I'm walking in yours."

Transparency in our family relationships is a God-given variable which He uses to make us authentic. Homeschool moms are rarely able to disguise how they spend any "free moments." Our children are, indeed, watching everything we do and are evaluating whether we do what we say. They appreciate openness, and will accept nothing less than honesty. If we cannot welcome this "glass-house" accountability, we need to at least accept it as inevitable. A writer once said : "The teaching that impacts is not from head to head, it is from heart to heart. It is a total personality, transformed by the supernatural grace of God, reaching out to transform other total personalities by the same grace." As we grow in transparency, we will change the hearts of our children to be more vulnerable and teachable.

The key to raising independent learners is to teach them to take responsibility for their learning. In essence, the lesson they learn is that it is not my responsibility to teach, it is their responsibility to learn. We perpetuate our children's immaturity by continuing to do tasks that should be their responsibilities.

As you release control of certain aspects in your children's lives, it is very important to assign parameters or boundaries. Children are insecure when they do not know who is in charge, or worse still, when the one in charge is an unpredictable, immature child. They want the security of structure, and someone who will back it up. One of the boundaries of behavior at our house is: if there was ever a fight over a toy, we *threw the toy away*. Some of you reading this may think that punishment is too severe, but I disagree. If we are teaching our children to value God and family above all else, we need to make it clear that *things* are not important—relationships are. A comforting result: we actually had to throw away only one or two big toys before the children *got* it and treated their siblings with respect.

When there was a true offense, the one who offended was to say these four things: I was wrong. I'm sorry. I love you. Will you forgive me? This is incredibly humbling, and Tim and I have also used it with each other and in our counseling.

Anne, from Kansas, is a homeschool mom of four grown children and ten grandchildren. She has always stressed the importance of allowing God to take our inability to forgive and replace it with His perfect forgiveness. Because of her diligence and sacrifice, her children are all now involved in serving God through the Armed Services, politics, service organizations, and in raising their godly families. One of her favorite verses is Psalm 126:3: "The Lord has done amazing things for us, and we are glad."

Whining was pretty much forbidden in our home. This truly is a choice of behavior, and you can modify that with appropriate punishment. The omission of whining alone can create a warm, comfortable environment in which to live this homeschooling lifestyle.

We also ruled that they could never ask for friends to come over in front of those friends. This taught them self-discipline and saved the embarrassment of explaining why we might not spend time with that particular friend. These behavioral boundaries are important as our children grow into the mature adults they can become.

We need to ask, "What responsibilities can my child assume that will be good not only for the rest of the family but will increase my child's sense of belonging today and equip him to be fully responsible in the future?" As you increase their financial, familial, and educational responsibilities, the message you are sending to them is: *We love you. We trust you. We want to help you as you learn to accept more and more responsibility for your own life.* These are three distinct areas in which we are charged with training, and then releasing, our children. Familial responsibilities revolve around those chores and jobs each child must perform within the family. I used to believe that you assigned a job to a child based on the age-appropriate readiness of each child. In a way, that is valid, but I would add one more suggestion: assign chores based on what needs *completing* in each child. For example, if your child is not very diligent about finishing a project, then you might give him the job of mowing the yard—with the condition that the job is not finished until the weed-eating is done—or until Dad approves.

Grow in Responsibility

God uses my husband, my children, and other relationships to smooth out my rough edges. I have to take responsibility for my growth. The more I change, the more I become an instrument of change in the lives of others.

We need to accept the fact that we are responsible for our own intellectual growth. This involves me fighting against my nature, which tells me constantly that "I need a break!" My children are watching me constantly and consistently—under a microscope.

It has been said that the only catalysts of growth after the age of twenty-five are the books we read and the people we meet. I believe that the person in the form of the Holy Spirit loves to help us grow. But I need to be careful of the things I read. For example, every magazine is composed of approximately 80 percent advertisements!   The whole ad industry exists to make us discontent with what we have and to entice us to want more— and better. Be selective in your choices and realize your choices have consequences.

Good books are the enemies of the *best* books. Pray for time to read for yourself and grow. There will be seasons of relaxing and refreshing—and books will change your perspective. Most times, I have three books that I am reading: one that I *want* to read, one that I *need* to read, and one that I *should* read. After I read one of the "ought-to's," I reward myself with the one I want to read. (It works for me because I believe in bribes—for me *and* my children.)

Expose yourself to people who stretch you—who cause you to think—who make you appreciate where God has you. Do not make the mistake of comparing yourself with others who have different giftings. Perspective can lighten our load, keep us from complaining, and enable us to live with a grateful heart.

Grow in Life skills

I help teach a day-long seminar to enable moms to teach their own children at home through high school. Linda, a homeschool mom of five, helped me develop this workshop, and added this priceless list of life skills, which she wanted her children to know before they graduated high school.

• Display godly character
• Wash/dry/fold laundry
• Cook a simple meal; set table
• Understand nutrition
• Cleaning: wash dishes/sweep/vacuum/clean bathroom
• Sew by hand and by machine
• Basic car maintenance: pump gas, check oil and tire pressure, and change tire
• Change, feed, and care for a baby
• Take responsibility for a pet's welfare
• Know simple first aid
• Yard maintenance
• Play musical instrument
• Money management: keep checking account/pay bills/budget/ taxes/tithe
• Typing
• Computer skills
• Phone skills
• Organizational skills

A mom of two homeschooled grown children gives this advice:

> By the time each child is twelve, they should be able to wash, dry, fold, and put in the correct place their own clothes. I started out when they were six and eight by having them place their folded clothes in boxes that I kept in the laundry room with their names on them. At night before bed, they would get their box, empty it in their drawers and replace the box in the laundry room. By the time they were eleven and thirteen, they were able to complete the entire task.

God is faithful to grow us up in His timing. He will give you insights as to which strategies might work for you now, and which ones you may need to incorporate later. If you journal, you will see the amazing growth in you and your children as you submit to His perfect guidance.

What does a normal day look like?

When I speak at conferences, I am frequently asked, "What does a normal day look like?" This question can be answered so many ways. One fact is that yearly, monthly, and sometimes weekly, "normal" changes. Most of the moms who ask this want a sense of validation—to see if they are "doing it right." What is right for me and my family cannot possibly be exactly right for you and your family. God will lead each of us to what works for our family *now*.

Having said that, I do like to give an overview of what a typical day might include. Keep in mind that I am a "type A" person and that my background was in education. I have always felt more secure with structure than with "unschooling" (letting our interests at any time dictate our study for that day). I also prefer an established curriculum as my "backbone," and then use my freedom to insert specific books, unit studies, or manipulatives to individualize each child's instruction. Factually, I can give you an hour-by-hour breakdown of a day we might experience in the lower grades through around eighth grade. (High school will entail more time, projects, work, and independent study.)

Breakfast & chores finished
8:00   Bible, memorization, word games
8:45   Read-alouds and math
9:30   Phonics, spelling, grammar
10:15 Short break
10:30 History and/or science
11:00 Logic, building thinking skills, reading comprehension
Lunch

I liken the entire process of how I homeschool to one of growing a garden. Figuratively, the planting, weeding, harvesting, and enjoying of a garden is a better picture of what a normal day should resemble. Each of these four major aspects of growing a garden is essential to the composition of my homeschool strategy.

Every year that we don't have a wedding in our family (recently we had three in four years!), we have a large vegetable garden. In order to ensure success, we spend much time discussing what specific kinds of fruits and vegetables we want to grow, the work involved, the quantities we desire, and the way these delicacies can be preserved to enjoy later. All four factors have to be investigated, weeded through, and agreed upon. If you do not have a target, you aim at nothing!

PLANTING
    After deciding and choosing which crops we want to grow, we have to purchase either the seeds or the young seedlings to start our garden. The entire area has to be tilled, disked, and fertilized. Before any growth can occur, the ground must be *prepared*.
    The research and planting process can be tedious and back-

breaking, but *nothing* can proceed without it. In our school day, this involves evaluating each child's strengths, his readiness, and the successes and failures of the previous year. I have to research on-line, in catalogs, and at curriculum fairs for materials. I seek counsel from other moms who may have used a certain curricula and/or have a similar family structure. I choose the materials best suited for each child—and best suited for what I desire the end result to be. I map out the first semester's objectives for each child—and pray for God's blessing.

WEEDING

Weeding a garden seems to be never-ending. As soon as I think that I have gotten every weed out of that half acre, the weeds start growing again where I began. But, if left untended, the plants will never reach their potential. They will die or be stunted by the bad weeds which steal their nutrients.

The same is true for teaching and correcting concepts in my homeschool. It is my responsibility to lay a proper foundation and to keep bad habits and undesirable character traits from overtaking their academic growth. Sloppiness, laziness, apathy, inconsiderateness, and arrogance are just a few of the growth-killers we have to weed out. The painstaking teaching of phonics rules, math facts, and memory lists are a daily necessity. You must go over them again and again, and even when you believe your child has mastered them, it is time for *review*. This is truly a weeding-out of the unnecessary and a replacing with that which leads to life and growth.

HARVESTING

In my vegetable garden, the amount of harvest depends on several things: how much was planted, the preparedness of the soil, the lack of predators, and God's natural gifts of sunshine and rain. This year we actually erected an electric fence around the entire half acre—one strand up high to keep out the deer, and one low for the raccoons. This worked and gave us much greater quantities than in previous years. During the height of the season, we had to pick the ripe veggies every other day, or we would risk overgrown, tasteless food.

In our homeschool, harvesting can be measured in daily or weekly tests, goals met, and love of learning inspired. You must develop specific criteria to ascertain if there is indeed growth. I had my children tested with a standardized national test every year—not for the state requirements, but for me. This gave me an indication of what still needed to be taught. However, each child is unique with his own giftings and his own timing of readiness. Therefore, I would never stress over a child receiving an average or below average evaluation for a topic one year. I would take into account his age, his readiness, that specific subject, and that particular school year. Our goal is mastery—on the *child's* timetable and not an artificial school schedule.

ENJOYING

As I write this, I am in the midst of cooking, canning, freezing, and drying our abundant garden. I have canned and frozen around a hundred quarts of food this summer. I have developed three new salsa recipes and tried making dill pickles for the first time (I am still learning!).

Last week, I thawed one quart of our sweet corn for a big family dinner. It was wonderful, and has given me a glimpse of how much we are going to enjoy this fresh-tasting corn in the dead of winter. If I could hold out a picture to you of how much you are going to enjoy the fruits of your labor, I would. This book is meant to be a beacon of encouragement to tell you that the harvest will be beyond your imagination. You will spend years planning and planting, correcting and weeding, evaluating and preserving, but it will be worth the work!

7

Appreciate

"I can live two months on one good compliment."

—Mark Twain

When we begin our homeschool day with prayer, we need to praise more than we petition. The word *appreciate* means to esteem highly. Our lifelong goal is to live out how we esteem our Lord.

Our children must learn to show appreciation for the many blessings and privileges they have been given. This is a taught behavior and is mandatory for homeschoolers. The last thing this world needs is arrogant, self-entitled geniuses who believe the world revolves around what they want and need.

In our early years of homeschooling, I struggled mightily with how to model true compassion and appreciation for our children. I felt woefully inconsiderate and selfish, and really could not imagine how God could make that character trait real in our lives. Not long after that prayer, we opened our home to an elderly, disabled gentleman from our church we had known and loved. In addition to teaching us all compassion and service, God showed us a man who was content in all things—a man who had truly learned to appreciate.

In recent years, I have seen the phenomenon of many large homeschooling families adopting more children. In our case, we "adopted"—but not another child. We adopted another grandfather.

Dock Duke was an elderly man we met at church. Over the years, we grew to love one another, and our two oldest boys spent many weekends in his company. With him, they not only experienced things we didn't have at home (TV and sugared cereals), but they helped him with his "truck farming" business (as the name implies, this is a farmer who grows fruits and vegetables at his home and then sells them out of his truck).

His life was one of unconditional love and sacrifice. He dropped out of school after third grade to help support his family. When he was old enough to "court," he was forced to put his life on hold to raise his two nephews. He was a wonderful father to them, and they are fine men today, singing his praises. After they graduated, his parents' health began to fail, and he stayed with and nursed them until their deaths.

In his seventies, while he was still living and farming at home, he was involved in a serious mower accident. He later recounted that he knew God had saved his life: A biker, who made the same routine trek up the highway by Dock's house, saw him under the mower and thought he was working on it. He waved at Dock, and assumed that Dock's reciprocal waves were of a friendly, and not frantic, nature, and so he biked on. Later down the road, this man was convicted that Dock was in trouble, and promptly turned around. When he saw Dock's injuries, he almost passed out, until Dock said, "Don't faint on me, Buddy, I need you to call 911." His life was saved, but his injuries and subsequent diabetes made him a risk for his landlord, and he was evicted. His family wanted to place him in a nursing home (of which he was terrified), so we offered for him to live with us. We had twelve delightful years together, and loved him like a family member. An article that was written for his funeral sums up the sacrificial, appreciative life this man lived.

Herbert Rudolph "Dock" Duke was born April 29, 1915, in Dickson, Tennessee. By the time Dock had completed grammar school, the family was in Williamson County, and Dock had begun a working/friendship relationship with the Murray Bush family that would last a lifetime. Dock began farming and later drove a "bait route" that let him travel through Middle Tennessee supplying worms and minnows to bait stores.

In the early fifties, Dock moved with his parents to a log house owned by the Bush family on Old Charlotte Rd. In 1954, seventeen-month-old nephew, Eddie, and four-day-old nephew, Freddie, came to live with Dock, and his parents, Caster and Floy.

Dock responded to the challenge of helping to raise his nephews by becoming the ultimate uncle/mentor. Freddie and Eddie recall learning to hunt, fish, swim, play baseball, and drive with Dock.

In 1963, on his way home from work one Wednesday afternoon, Dock drove past Forest Home Church of Christ, noticed that the church was hosting a "tent meeting" and proceeded home to inform the family that they would all be going to the church meeting that evening. From that day on, Forest Home Church and the Christian walk was a priority to the Duke family. Dock became a teacher and leader at the church and occasionally had to reach deep into his own pockets to pay the bills and the preacher. Dock continued to live with and care for his parents until Floy died in 1977 and Caster followed in 1978.

In 1980, my husband and I began worshiping at Forest Home. Dock did his best to spoil our children, regularly taking Will and Gil to McDonald's after church and to Wal-Mart for toys and candy. In 1991, after a lawn tractor accident, it seemed Dock, now seventy-six, could not live independently, so the families at Forest Home took up a collection to "raise a room" on the back of our house, and Dock moved in. For the next twelve years, Dock lived with his adopted family and took pleasure in gardening, splitting kindling, visiting with his family and friends, swinging on his porch swing, and spoiling Will, Gil, and Danielle, his little buddy Luke, and all the children at Forest Home.

Dock's wealth consisted not of possessions, but of the love and respect of all who knew him, and perhaps the rarest of treasures: contentment and peace. Several times he said, "I have never worried a day in my life."

Although Dock never married or fathered children, he allowed God to use him to help influence his nephews and many others and to care for his parents. Later, when Dock needed caring for, God, in His faithfulness, provided a place for him to live with a family who loved him dearly. Now Dock lives in a mansion prepared for him by Jesus Himself.

Dock will be missed by his family, his church family, his "adopted family," and many friends until, by God's grace, we will see him later.

A concrete way for homeschool moms to teach appreciation is by modeling this character trait. Your children need to hear you verbally express appreciation for their dad—when he is there and when he is not there. Your children need to hear from your lips how special they are to God—and to you.

Almost every time I speak, I get a question or comment on how involved dads should be in the home education process. My answer remains the same. Each homeschool dad is working the equivalent of *two* jobs so that you can stay home and teach your children! The last thing he needs is for you to lay a guilt trip on him that "So-and-So's husband is helping teach all their children math." *If* a husband is gifted and inclined to offer to teach a subject, you should not necessarily turn it down, but it is not his responsibility! Please appreciate the job he is doing to allow you to follow this wonderful calling.

Be creative in how you model appreciation. Some families have each child verbally affirm a sibling at dinner each night. You may be amazed at how quickly the sibling rivalry will diminish if you practice this discipline.

Because we homeschool moms are always haunted by the "not doing enough" specter, we need all the appreciation and encouragement possible. On a certain Mother's Day when our finances were very low, I made gingerbread cookies for my mom. Since I am the oldest of five, I wrote this poem to give to her:

We are five little gingerbread men
Who are made from sugar and spice
We are molded and shaped and baked on a shelf

And everyone says we're quite nice

But real children are made of much more than spice
God cut the pattern himself
And children are nurtured and cherished and loved
And never ignored on a shelf

This recipe calls for years, fears, and tears
The baker asks not for reward
But sees the fruits of her labor
In each child's love of the Lord

We dedicate this day to one
Whom children owe everything to
For the molding and shaping of each little heart
Only a MOTHER can do.

It has been said that instant availability without continuous presence is probably the best role a mother can play. Much can be said about the self motivation and independent mindset needed to succeed in homeschooling. Parents must learn to differentiate and find a balance between the constant nurturing of and the releasing of their children. It may take years for your children to comprehend your devotion and sacrifice and begin to show appreciation, but it will happen. A homeschooled junior in high school was asked, "What is the best thing about homeschooling?" He said, "When my mom leaves me alone." The next question put to him was, "So, what is the worst thing about homeschooling?" He thoughtfully replied, "When my mom leaves me alone."

Anne Ortlund said, "Expect God to speak differently to them than He does to you. They are being prepared for a later world you won't be a part of; His plans for them are specialized. Let them go, and understand you can't follow. Tell them, 'The more I sense you're getting orders from God, the less I'll tell you what to do. And I'm delighted to hand you over to Him. Soon my job will be over, and you'll just be following Him. I'll let God take over, and you'll be in perfect hands forever."

Whether we like it or not, we moms are the climate controllers in our homes. If we are worried, faithless, unappreciative, and insecure, it *will* be borne out in the day of our husbands and children. As we grow to show appreciation to our family, they will be motivated to return the favor. However, we must always look to God for our "pats on the back." He is the One we must please, and He will encourage us with His perfect appreciation. Isaiah 51:1–2 says, "Listen to me you who pursue righteousness—who seek the Lord—look to the rock from which you were hewn."

When our daughter was in a Bible class at a Christian university, she had to write a paper which epitomizes the topic of appreciation. The title was "Ten Things My Parents Did Right":

1. They encouraged Christ in every aspect of my life.
2. Honesty—My parents have always been honest with me. Even when they were having marriage problems, they did not try to hide anything from me.
3. Support—My parents are supportive of my decisions, even if it meant going to school six hours away.
4. Involvement—My parents went to every athletic event, music recital, etc. that I ever had.
5. Verbally express their love for me—They do this not because of what I do, but because of who I am.
6. Strong emphasis on family—I have a very close relationship with my parents, brothers, and extended family.
7. They placed little importance on money or material wealth.
8. Education—My parents sacrificed a lot to educate my brothers and me at home.
9. They showed me clear family roles—My mom and dad respect each other, but my mom is in submission to my dad. My dad worked hard to provide for my family so that my mom could stay home and educate my family.
10. Relaxed fun and hospitality—Our house is always open for guests and friends to hang out. I cannot remember a summer that we did not have at least one extra person living with us.

Anita, a homeschool mom in Iowa, says:

> Phillip's first job at sixteen was at a daycare center, where most boys his age wouldn't think of working. At age ten, John befriended a boy, Alex, whose twin brother, Brian, had cerebral palsy. The mom was surprised that John invited the handicapped brother to come play also. She called me to warn me— *Did we know that Brian was handicapped?* To John, it was normal life: brothers always hung out together, no matter what age or handicap. The three would go to a golf course with one bag of clubs to share. Brian was given time to golf as he could. We found out years later from a newspaper article that Brian continued to play golf. He is now in a golf league with people who are handicapped, and the article was congratulating him for receiving the first place trophy that year. It was mentioned that he enjoyed golf because it was something he could do alone or with those that chose to play with him. The experience of relating to all ages and valuing each person as God created them was learned through homeschooling and is used by them daily as they work, and in their personal lives.

When we offer ourselves up to God to serve Him in whatever way He should ask, His will can be worked through us to *His* glory. To whatever degree we refuse to surrender, and give in to selfishness, this limits our ability to serve God. Our Savior is not committed to our happiness. Instead, Jesus is committed to His Father's plan, which involves surrender.

Yield to the fact that no parent does a perfect job. Concede to the understanding that we'll never get to spend all the time with each other that we want. Surrender to the reality that we cannot be all things to all people in our lives—especially all at once. Appreciate where God has you.

In America today, we cannot fully appreciate the freedoms we enjoy. The absolute freedom to teach our own children is such a privilege! As God calls us deeper into His will for our lives, we should reflect on and appreciate the place we have in history with regard to the home education movement.

I want to end this chapter with a re-telling of the true story of some courageous pioneers who fought with everything they had to secure the blessing of freedom for their families. In 1843, there were 120 covered wagons which started out on the Oregon Trail. These were not the first covered wagons to make the trip, but the first ones to take families. There were 260 men and 610 children.

They were up by 4 a.m., awakened by the "alarm" of a rifle. The men rounded up the cattle and horses, while the children dressed. Breakfast was cooked and eaten, tents taken down and readied, and mules and oxen rigged to go. They were ready to move on at seven o'clock.

Why were they making this impossibly dangerous journey? They had heard tales and visions of a land west founded on freedom, where there were "valleys so fertile even the fence posts sprouted fruit." They were propelled along by written journals of the first explorers who had made it successfully. These served as a "self-help" guide to the wilderness, with details of the best route through the mountains.

These pioneers had many tough decisions to weigh. The cost of the journey was high. Many gave up and sold homes, and they all surrendered and sacrificed to afford the trip.

The covered wagon represented the simplest living and traveling environment. The wagon was termed a "prairie schooner." This wagon carried everything the family would need to live, including a plow, ax, hammer, shovel, cooking utensils, 200 pounds of flour, 10 pounds of salt, 25 pounds of sugar, medicine, guns, lead for bullets, and spare wagon parts.

Many had a choice for the animal which pulled their wagon. Mules were faster but they often quit under heavy loads. Oxen were the best choice since they cost less, ate the available prairie grass, and most importantly, were able to travel the entire way.

These pioneers needed to wait for the perfect time to begin their journey. If they started too soon in the year, the oxen would not find enough grass to eat and they would die. If they waited too late in the year, the pioneers risked being caught in the relentless winter season.

On a good day of travel, as many as twenty miles could be completed. On bad days, they would encounter storms and hard winds. This would slow their trip, but they pressed on and still proceeded. Each morning on the road, vital routines were followed obediently. Cows were milked, and the milk was placed in pails which were tied onto the wagon. As the pails were jostled with the hard bumps of the wilderness road, the milk was churned into delicious cream and butter.

Indians often approached the wagon train. Some were friendly and curious and let the travelers go on their way. Some tribes desired to steal from them, causing the men to circle the wagons to protect their families. As one means of protection, they formed a simple government. The members agreed to set and abide by rules for the good of the whole community. They set aside their own personal differences and grievances to reach their goal harmoniously.

Life on the trail was incredibly hard; the pioneers were surrounded by casualties. Many of their women and children died en route. Even their animals were decimated. Their journal told of one such incident where a stampede of 3,000 buffalo plunged over a precipice into a raging river where scores of them drowned. On Windlass Hill, the slope was so steep that they had to rope their wagons together and use their collective weight to keep from hurtling to their destruction.

When they reached a "narrow ridge with a gorge 1,000 feet down on the left and a sheer precipice on the right down to the Snake River," they called it "The Devil's Backbone." Here, it was necessary to lighten their loads by jettisoning some of their most treasured possessions. Thus the trail became a winnowing process and test of what the pioneers valued most.

Along the trail, they arrived at Fort Bridger, a resting way station. They recognized this as a place of safety and renewal. Here, they refitted their old wagon wheels and traded their exhausted oxen for fresh ones. They also shared vital life-saving information with other visiting travelers regarding directions, unfriendly natives, and upcoming weather reports.

Days later, they reached Willamette Valley, Oregon. There was marked a simple diary notation: "Friday, October 27, Arrived at Oregon City. Saturday, October 28, Went to work." One out of 17 who set foot on that trail perished from disease or accidents. They had a motto: "The cowards never started and the weak died on the way."

Almost 170 years later, we are the first generation home education leaders. We are pioneers. We are up early—around seven o'clock—children are dressed, beds made, breakfast cooked and eaten, and teaching resources are prepared.

Why are we making this impossibly hard journey? We know that there are reports of freedom in education where children "are eager to drink up knowledge and sprout good fruits." We are propelled along by the written works of the first American homeschoolers. They have made it successfully and have written precise details of the best route through the daily mountains and valleys of life.

We have many tough decisions to weigh. The cost is high. We have to give up unrealistic expectations, and learn to daily surrender and sacrifice our time and energy to make this journey.

We understand that success will come with the simplest learning environment: warm fellowship, conversation, reading aloud, and teaching how to serve others. We desire to do things *with* our children rather than *at* them.

We have many choices of teaching resources. Some will keep our children busier but will burn them out quickly. As we research, we find others that cost less, are available, and consistently lead us onward.

We have to wait for the perfect timing to begin any learning endeavor. If we start too early, it can lead to painful burnout and the death of a desire for learning. If we wait too late, we risk getting caught in ensconced bad habits and boredom.

On good days, much ground is covered. On others, storms of doubt and laziness rage. We still proceed, one step at a time, toward our goal. Each morning, we obediently go through routines of discipline and learning. We find that sometimes the interruptions and hard knocks of our journey turn the routines into something beautiful—and useful.

Those who are foreign to home education approach us. Some are friendly and curious. Others desire to steal our joy and capture us as slaves into a hostile system. Then, we need to "circle our wagons" and work to protect our families. Sometimes we need to set aside our differences to reach our educational goals harmoniously.

We are surrounded by homeschool casualties. We encounter skeletons of former homeschoolers who perished for lack of proper nourishment and support. Children's imaginations are dying from lack of intellectual creativity. Sometimes in our fight against unrelenting irrational educational bureaucrats, we need to rope together and use our collective weight to get things done in the lobbying effort. We need to unite to lead others effectively and to keep all of us from drowning in unnecessary legislation.

When we have "days from Hades" where we feel we are surrounded by impossibilities, we have to lighten our loads by throwing off all but the most essential. This is truly a leaving behind—a winnowing process of the soul and a test of what we value most.

When we read a book like this one, we recognize it as a safe place of rest and renewal. Here, you can re-think old teaching methods and trade in tired ideas for fresh ones. You can read vital information from other home educators regarding the best routes, unfriendly upcoming legislation, and life-saving encouragement.

Many who set out to home educate perish from ignorance or accidents. The cowards never started and the weak died along the way. Our lesson planners need to read with simplicity: "Daily—taught my children as I am called to do." Nearly 170 years after the first pioneers blazed the Oregon Trail, you can still see the wheel impressions in the earth. In the generations to come, if the Lord waits, will the impressions you leave lead others on their path to freedom?

8

Serve

"Life is either a daring adventure or nothing at all."

—Helen Keller

Second Timothy 2 states that "with this body of truth, I am building this into your life. Now I charge you to take that same truth and deposit it into the lives of others, teaching them in a way that they will be equipped to teach others."

We homeschoolers can be downright self-righteous sometimes. In addition to assuming that our educational choices are always superior to everyone else's, we can develop "tunnel-vision." By that, I mean that we choose to neglect every other ministry out there because our days are filled with homeschooling. I will be the first to tell you that the decision to homeschool does involve significant sacrifice, and many trivial hobbies and occupations will effectively be discarded. This is a natural progression of the parent taking full responsibility for the education of her children.

However, if our home revolves exclusively around our children, we have our priorities out of proportion. The only message we then send to our children is that they are entitled and worthy of all our time and sacrifice; they will become self-absorbed and all important in their own eyes. Homeschool should be a tool that God uses to bring about what He wants to happen in your entire family. It is one part of the wheel that rotates according to His pleasure!

Elizabeth, a homeschooling mom of four from Tennessee, felt that service was of utmost importance:

> We wanted to instill a heart of service in our children. Besides short-term mission trips, our children were involved in serving at the Nashville Rescue Mission, CareNet, decorating soldiers' graves for the VFW, putting on Thanksgiving programs for recovery ministries, and in state-wide and local home education organizations. They also assisted with the new construction of a local church.

She has now seen the fruit of her labors. Her grown children all serve the Lord and their families. Because she persevered in teaching them, her children are disciplined and tender-hearted and the child least interested in high school science is now graduating from medical school.

We need to say, "Father, please show me how to go out into Your world and glorify You." This is essentially the opposite of being self-centered. Only those who are secure in the true source of their power and strength are capable of servanthood. They serve because they are free to do so.

Obviously, we homeschoolers invest in people rather than programs and projects. We pour out our lives in service to our children. However, we must teach our children to serve others. We are sending them as a living message to a time we'll never see. We should hold as vitally important the desire to inspire this next generation to follow God more implicitly. What an audacious hope! As we serve our families in this area, we hope to pass on this example of radically following God—no matter what.

Calvin Miller, in speaking of the nature of a true servant leader, pointed out some essentials. He said, "To be a true servant leader, you really need two things: a flashlight and an index finger. The light keeps it from being dark, and the finger points the way." We have to lead by example in serving. We must teach our children that service to God is our calling. Obviously, Jesus taught that serving is the only way to greatness—we want our children to be great, don't we?

Because homeschoolers have an efficient way of imparting knowledge, we need to accept the fact that we will be called to greater service. With privilege comes responsibility. Each family must evaluate their calling, their interests, and the number and ages of children, and decide where their time will best be spent in service. Obviously, serving your extended family comes first, followed closely by serving with your local church's ministries. A word of caution, however, to those of you serving in large churches: the staff in large churches attempts to place children in segregated age groups, believing this to be easier for them to accommodate with adult helpers. We have seen much greater spiritual success when families adopt a service project together rather than splintering your own personal work force. As with reading books aloud, there is a tangible "something" when you experience serving a greater cause *together*.

Beyond your church ministries, there is much validity in committing your children to pray for God's leading in which place to serve. Friends of ours listened carefully to their oldest daughter's heart for adopting babies in China, and this family is now responsible for over 2,000 Chinese babies being rescued from orphanages. Have your children keep a prayer journal, and ask them to share what they feel God is telling them as the first part of your school day. Do not allow any sibling to belittle or downplay their growing vision. Embrace hard enterprises as a family, and you will be amazed at what God can do!

As with so many of these success strategies, listen for God's leading—and be creative. Many of us have church ministries in which we are involved. Some of these are worth the outlay of time, but some are not. Only by each family member praying can you ascertain where God wants you. Beware of time-intensive youth programs which separate the teens from the parents for an inordinate amount of time each week. This can be very counter-productive for a homeschooler. There can be much emphasis on dating and other past-times to which your family may object.

Many homeschooling families throughout the nation choose short-term mission trips to serve others. YWAM, Habitat for Humanity, Samaritan's Purse, Casas por Christos, and inner city rehabilitation are other examples. Local nursing homes and hospitals always need volunteers. Our daughter, who is now a nurse, actually found her calling when she first volunteered at our county hospital.

Many veterinary hospitals like to use students during the school year when their college helpers are away. Check around your church to find opportunities for mentoring or apprentice-ship. Allow your children to volunteer at libraries or hospice houses. Let both boys and girls learn life skills at your church's Mother's Day Out.

A busy mom of five added this wisdom for choosing a place for her children to serve:

> I realize this is probably not the "norm," but our family hasn't been big on choosing one organization or time of year to volunteer. It has always bugged me tremendously to see how generous "Christians" get at Thanksgiving and Christmas— when, in fact, people go hungry and live on the streets all year long!
>
> Having a servant's heart is vitally important, so... instead, we are trying to show our children how to find simple, every-day ways to minister and bless others. I want them to notice the world around them. I want them to be aware of that exhaust-ed-looking lady across the parking lot who has just pushed a buggy of tired, screaming children to her car and still has to somehow find the strength to get her groceries in the car and her buggy back to the stall.
>
> I want them to realize that the older lady down the road wants *her* yard to look nice too. And with her son living out of state and her husband being so sick, it just isn't going to hap-pen unless somebody takes the time to help her get it done. I want them to understand that sometimes "payment" comes in

the form of a glass of lemonade and a kind word of appreciation. Looking at this, I am forced to realize that these things
are nothing I can add to their portfolio, but then again, getting
them into college isn't my number one priority. Getting them
into heaven is.

AMEN!!

The homeschool organization which serves the area where
you live is an excellent place to begin volunteering. Our experience is that most of these are run by busy homeschool moms
who are trying to also teach their children in their spare time! As
a mom, *you* also need to volunteer to bless others. As you seek to
teach your children to serve, be aware that their education comes
first—with very few exceptions. Learn to balance your service
with moderation.

A preacher called at the home of a very poor family in a run-
down shack. When he came out, he found one of the family's
two daughters admiring his new car. The minister explained that
he had received it as a gift from his sister. Now, most of us hearing this would say, "I wish *I* had a sister like that." However, this
young lady said, "I sure wish that I could *be* a sister like that."

9

Laugh

"I'm sure the reason such young nitwits are produced in our schools is because they have no contact with anything of any use in everyday life."
—Petronius (circa 66) [Notice the date—I'm not saying anything about *your* public schools!]

"A keen sense of humor helps us to overlook the unbecoming, understand the unconventional, tolerate the unpleasant, overcome the unexpected, and outlast the unbearable."
—Billy Graham

For those of you just beginning the homeschool journey, laughter must seem like such an odd choice for a success strategy. From a novice's standpoint, you might assume that each school day (or week) would naturally be full of fun and laughter. You might believe that laughter would be a by-product of living and learning together.

However, for those of us in the trenches of learning problems, multi-level ages, scope and sequence deadlines, and sibling rivalry, that could not be farther from the truth. Laughter is too often the most neglected part of our curriculum. This strategy could possibly be the most important one to add to your day!

I have written this chapter as a microcosm of how each school day should "play out." Some of my favorite jokes to tell home-schoolers are interspersed between the following paragraphs. In the same way, laughter should surround and intersperse our days as we mold, shape, and *enjoy* our young ones.

Truisms that five-year-olds learn:
1. You can't trust dogs to watch your food.
2. No matter how hard you try, you can't baptize cats.
3. When your mom is mad at your dad, don't let her brush your hair.

Jesus had one purpose—to obey His Father's will. But His life revolved around that purpose in a balanced way. We know He took time to sleep, to eat, and to fellowship with friends. He encouraged His disciples to rest, and He joined them. He always encouraged joy. John 10:10 says, "I have come that you may have life and have it to *the full*" (emphasis mine).

A woman carried a baby into the doctor's examining room. The doctor arrived, examined the baby, checked his weight, and found it below normal. The doctor asked if the baby was breast- or bottle-fed. The woman replied, "Breast-fed." The doctor instructed the woman, "Well, strip to your waist." She complied. The doctor then proceeded to press, knead, roll, cup, and pinch both breasts in a detailed, rigorously thorough examination.

Motioning for her to get dressed, he said, "Well, no wonder this baby is underweight. You don't have any milk!" "I know," she said, "I'm his grandmother; but I'm glad I came."

When our son Will was thirteen, he seemed to major in rolling his eyes at me. I will be the first to admit that I *am* corny, but sometimes that "smart-aleck" age can be hard to bear. During this time frame, I had a good friend who was having doubts about her ability to begin home education. She seemed to think that our homeschooling was easy.

She said, "But, Karen, I know you! I bet you make everyday in homeschooling so *fun!*"

Knowing that Will would be apt to throw cold water on that statement (I actually pictured him falling down on the floor laughing), I replied, "Why don't you ask Will that question?"

When she did, you almost had to pick *me* up off the floor. In my mind, I looked back over the last several months of school, and it seemed to me to consist of drudgery, discipline, and much eye-rolling. Imagine my surprise when Will said, "Well, not *every* day is fun, but most of them."

I believe that God is in the business of redeeming and multiplying. He multiplies talents...and joy. He magnifies the fun times we have in homeschool, and that overshadows and minimizes the boring parts.

A redneck family from the hills was visiting the city, and they were in a mall for the first time in their lives. The father and son were strolling around while the wife shopped. They were amazed by almost everything they saw, but especially by two shiny, silver walls that could move apart and slide back together again. The boy asked, "Pa, what's 'at?" The father (never having seen an elevator) responded, "Son, I dunno. I ain't never seen nothin' like that in my entire life. I ain't got no idea what it is." While the boy and his father were watching with amazement, a fat old lady in a wheelchair rolled up to the moving walls and pressed a button. The walls opened, and the lady rolled between them into a small room. The walls closed and the boy and his father watched the small numbers above the walls light up. Then the walls opened up again and a gorgeous and voluptuous twenty-four-year-old blond stepped out. Without taking his eyes off the young woman, the father said quietly to his son, "Boy, go git yer mama."

Educational games have always been a high priority in our school day. In a normal school day, after Bible, I would typically start the bookwork with a word puzzle, a cryptogram, or a riddle. We might then actually get down on the floor to play a board game. There are so many educational games out there. Check out Amazon.com, your local Christian bookstore, and your local parent-teacher store. One of my favorites to play with older children was called "Bethumped." This game was all about word origins and proper word usage, but it was *fun*.

Everyone knows who Bill Gates is—one of the richest men in the world, who dropped out of college and had a great idea about personal computing. In his book Business @ the Speed of Thought, *he argues that our feel-good, politically correct culture has created a generation of kids with no concept of reality. He believes that they are set up for failure in the "real world." He shares eleven rules of life that students never learn in school, but should.*

Bill Gates' Rules for Young People:

Rule 1 - Life is not fair, get used to it.
Rule 2 - The world won't care about your self-esteem. The world will expect you to accomplish something before *you feel good about yourself.*
Rule 3 - You will NOT make fifty thousand dollars a year right out of high school. You won't be a vice president with a Blackberry, either, until you earn both.
Rule 4 - If you think your teacher is tough, wait until you get a boss.
Rule 5 - Flipping burgers is not beneath your dignity. Your grandparents had a different word for burger flipping: they called it opportunity.
Rule 6 - If you mess up, it's not your parents' fault. Don't whine about your mistakes; instead, learn from them.

Rule 7 - Before you were born, your parents weren't as boring as they are now. They got that way from paying your bills, cleaning your clothes, and listening to how cool you are. So, before you save the rainforest from the pollution of your parents' generation, try cleaning up the clothes in your own room first.

Rule 8 - Your school may have done away with winners and losers, but life has not. In some schools they have abolished failing grades and they will let you try as many times as you want to get the right answer. This doesn't bear the slightest resemblance to anything in real life.

Rule 9 - Life is not divided into semesters. You don't get summers off, and very few employers are interested in helping you find yourself. Do that on your own time.

Rule 10 - Television is not real life. In real life people actually have to leave the coffee shop and go to their jobs.

Rule 11 - Be nice to nerds. Chances are you'll end up working for one.

Be creative in your methods of instruction. By this, I mean think outside the box in terms of location of instruction and reinforcement of lessons. Teach in a tree-house...on a boat...in a dark closet with flashlights...at midnight...on a quilt at the park. Use Silly String wars...food fights...blindfolds...Super Soaker contests...scavenger hunts.

Not long ago, soon after the opening of the large Atlanta aquarium, a friend of mine told me this true story about an acquaintance of hers.

This young mom from Alabama packed up her five-year-old son and drove the several-hour trip to visit the aquarium. Sometime during the course of their visit, she experienced that horrible feeling we have all felt, when, for just a second, we lose track of our children. After searching frantically, she told a security guard standing nearby that she could not find her son. He immediately radioed downstairs and the place was effectively locked down.

For the next long while, the mom and all the security force searched that area for her son. Despairing that someone had taken her child off the premises, she finally looked inside *the new penguin exhibit. There, oblivious to anything but the families of penguins, sat her son, playing happily. The mom, overwhelmed with such mixed emotions of relief and anger, grabbed her son up and hugged him fiercely. Apologizing profusely to the assembled personnel, she beat a hasty retreat to her car and made the long trip back to Alabama. On the way home, she told the boy that he was* so *in trouble for leaving her side and going where no one was allowed.*

"As soon as we get home, you are having a bath to wash all the dirt from the penguin pen off, and then you are getting a spanking!" She was so thankful, but also aware of how close they had come to tragedy.

They continued the long trip home.

Upon arriving, she pulled the shower curtain open and told her son to get in and get washed up before his spanking. She was busy folding clothes when she heard him laughing. That infuriated her: the thought that he was not aware of how dangerous his escapade had been. She flung open the curtain to further reprimand him, and could not believe what she saw: he was in the bathtub playing with a BABY PENGUIN!!

She grabbed up the phone and called the aquarium to tell how embarrassed she was, but that she could get in her car right then and bring the little penguin back. The officials told her to wait right there. Three hours later, several large refrigerated vehicles drove up to retrieve their precious belonging.

This little boy would be the poster child for homeschooling: always discovering and exploring!

Since traditions build strength in our families, choosing movies to watch as a family will lead to much laughter. This will necessitate much trial-and-error, but re-watching them is a certain indicator of success. Some of our family favorites would include: *The Five Mile Creek Gang*, all the Veggie Tales shows, many Muppets, UHF, the old Disney classics, *Swiss Family Robinson*, *Homeward Bound*, *Anne of Green Gables*, and many of the new Pixar films.

If corn oil is made from corn and vegetable oil is made from vegetables, what is baby oil made from?

Why do doctors leave the room while you change? They are going to see you naked anyway.

Written on a wall in the ladies room: "My husband follows me everywhere." Written just below that: "I do not."

Including your children in choices is so important as they grow older. At different times, let them choose their own unit study (from your master list), and let them take the initiative in choosing texts, field trips, and lesson reinforcement. When there is a sense of ownership, you will see an increased interest. Work *with* what is happening in the home, rather than against it. When Danielle and I were doing a unit study on early childhood education, we waited to schedule it until around Christmas, when her baby brother was due. Talk about hands-on curriculum! We did botany around our gardening season. We did a unit on organization to start the school year. Involve your children to make your school year fun.

In the last few years of the twelve we had with Dock, his health necessitated many hospital trips. The hospital is only twenty minutes from my house, but I am notorious for leaving my gas gauge near "E." So, it should have come as no surprise when, on one trip back home with Dock, I ran out of gas—within sight of a gas station. I did not want to pay an inflated amount for a gas

*can, so I looked everywhere in the car for a container to trans-
port just enough gas to get down the hill to the station. Dock and
I had packed up everything not nailed down in his hospital room
(after all, we paid for it). I remember hearing that gasoline can
be carried for a few minutes in a plastic bottle before the gases
become dangerous.*

*Well, I didn't have a plastic bottle, but I did have. . . a pink
plastic hospital bedpan. I went quickly to the gas station, put one
dollar's worth of gas into the bedpan and walked carefully back
to the car. As I was pouring the contents of the bedpan into our
gas tank, a fellow Franklinite slowed his car enough to yell out
of his window, "Now, that's faith!"*

Tim and I were able to help lead many families who were beginning to homeschool in the '80s. We helped to develop an organization which ministered to these families' needs. A part of
the package of services we offered to the homeschooling families
all across Tennessee was a subscription to a monthly magazine.
We named it *Jonathan's Arrow* for several reasons. The first is
that the purpose of an arrow is to point one to safety—to the
answer—to the right direction, and to point away from danger.
The name *Jonathan's Arrow* refers, of course, to the Jonathan in
the Old Testament, who shot an arrow for David, demonstrating
his love, loyalty, friendship, and steadfastness.

This magazine is still a wonderful help to families all over our
state. It includes articles of encouragement, curricula reviews by
veteran moms, notices of upcoming field trips and group classes,
and sports events. During our tenure, the editor came up with
the idea of a monthly column of "advice to the novice homeschooler" called "Dear Karen." Many of the questions were a
little tongue-in-cheek, but the queries behind them are very real
and relevant to moms now. I've included some here that were
published over the many years I wrote them.

Dear Karen,

It's now the end of March, and I've brought my children home from public school to homeschool. Should I buy books, work on attitude, or let them play and decide what they want to do? —**Undecided**

Dear Un,

Sorry, but there is no "one right answer" to your question. It really depends on your children. Are they excited about coming home, or resistant? Was there a traumatic event that precipitated your removing them from school? How prepared are you to suddenly take on the demands of their education?

All these factors and more play a part in your decision of what to do with the next few weeks. If your children are eager to be home and receptive to your instruction, go ahead, get your feet a little wet and work on a few subjects with each of them. Next year won't seem so intimidating. I would not spend a fortune on this year's books. With so little time left, I'd see what the library has or what you can borrow from friends with older kids.

On the other hand, if a damaging incident or series of events led you to bring your children home, they and you may need time to heal. Look at their emotional tanks. Are they full or dangerously low? There are many ways to learn without duplicating a formal school setting at home. Read aloud to your children. Go to interesting places. Turn them on to good books they can read for themselves. Give them time to get excited about learning again.

If a child is reluctant to receive instruction from you, spend this time working on your relationship and nurturing an attitude of learning. Spend sweet time together. Talk about things your child finds interesting. Try to spark discussion (not debate). Gently get them in the habit of listening to you and considering ideas you present. Though there is no single answer to everyone in your situation, prayerful consideration of the factors affecting your children will help you make a good decision for your family. Meanwhile, welcome to homeschooling!

Dear Karen,

We are a typically busy home educating family. We are over-involved in lots of good things. We are tired. We wonder if life is supposed to be this hectic. What do you do to ensure that you are not overwhelmed with "busy-ness"? —**Francis Frenzied**

Dear Francis,

In spite of all the things our family *does* do, in the past few years we have given up (or gotten out of) Girl Scouts, 4-H, all baseball and swim teams, some group classes, a soccer league, and chairing several functions. That is a lot to whittle down, but entirely necessary as our children grow older. Especially then there is a vital need to simplify and specialize. Pray to discern which activities are better left behind. You cannot do it all!

Give yourself credit for all the instruction, teaching, and discipline you do everyday, and give yourself a day (or at least a morning) off. Get out of the house (where your never-ending work ridicules and gloats at you) and go to Cheekwood (a local botanical garden) just to enjoy—not teaching. Or...hire a homeschooling teen or a mature pre-teen to come help you with piled-up housework or to keep the kiddoes while you tackle that one closet or corner. Sometimes small victories can ease the accumulated stress of clutter. We may feel overwhelmed because we are in the midst of chaos. Or...pick a day where the children are in charge of the educational process. Give them a few criteria, and let them create.

It sounds as though your whole family is tired: let your teens sleep late sometimes! Their growing bodies need extra rest (the best hours are before midnight, however). Since we never have "snow days," we sometimes have a "beautiful day" simply to relax and renew.

As you pare down, there is one thing which you need to add

to your life. You need to incorporate exercise into your daily routine to give you extra energy and stress relief. You will be amazed at the immediate results in your irritation plateau, your energy level, and your ability to manage stress. Simplify, change your routine, lighten up, and celebrate those children.

Dear Karen,

My child is 7 and doesn't really know how to read. Is this my fault or does he have a reading problem? Or is it something else? Can you help me?
Signed, **Worried Mom**

Dear Worried,

First of all, don't worry. Not all children read at age 5! I want to share a word from a friend of mine who has been where you are. I received a phone call last week from a home education mom whom I had not seen in years. Naturally, we reminisced a few minutes. As I told her our oldest is now a junior in high school (and still home taught), she laughed and reminded me of when he was five and I was in a panic that he didn't know a noun from a verb. You, too, laugh now, but let's be honest—plenty of you are in a frenzy because your eight-year-old can't read or your seven-year-old doesn't know Latin. Well, let me encourage you—don't get sucked into the myth that every child reads at the age of five or six—they don't. We have two sons: the oldest learned to read quite easily. However, he was eight or nine before I considered him "proficient," and the younger son struggled and did not read well until he was ten. Now, at age twelve, he lacks confidence. And this is difficult to admit, but he doesn't like to read. Can you imagine? Doesn't he realize he was born into a home education family and a love of reading is supposed to be natural? Here are some words of wisdom from someone who has been there, done that. First, be patient. Not just for the first year, but continue to be patient for however many years it takes your child to learn to read, or write, or perform whatever skill you are trying to teach them. Second, daily read out loud to your child, even after they learn to read on their own. Some kids actually dread learning to read for fear their mom or dad will no longer sit down and read to them. Third, read Dr. Raymond Moore's book, *Better Late than Early*, and any other book by Dr. Moore. (Also be sure to read *For the Children's Sake*, by Susan Schaeffer Macaulay, and *The Whole Hearted Child* by Clay Clarkson.) Fourth, use a simple phonics program. Save "language arts" for later. Fifth, and this is very important: Don't listen to advice from anyone who tells you their child started reading or did algebra or knew Newton's three Laws of Motion before the age of 10. This no-pressure philosophy frees you from a world of guilt and allows your child to progress at his own pace—not a pace set by someone else. "Subjects" may rob your child of their natural curiosity. Allow your child to know the people who made history, instead of a group of uninteresting dates. After all, 1776 means nothing without the people who made it what it is. And enjoy science. A formal science curriculum can easily wait until your child is at least 10. Yes, these are my opinions, but I formed them after twelve years of home education and countless discussions with other parents and even "professional" teachers. I encourage you—relax. Don't try to teach them everything before they're ten.

Dear Karen,

I have a first grader with a math "block." She enjoys math time but has difficulty with even the basics. Am I doing her a disservice to skip around using different curriculums and math "games," or should I stay with one curriculum (I use Miquon as primary curriculum) and do it until she gets it? I know we don't always want to compare our methods to other schooling methods, but how can I evaluate her abilities when I feel math is not my strong subject either? —**Pondering Paula**

Dear Pondering,

I think one of the beauties of all the resources available in curricula now is the freedom to "skip around" and choose. Of course, stability within structure is important to most learning styles, and obviously, there must be balance. But in the early grades, and especially in math, I highly recommend trial and error—learning what interests her, what inspires, what works. Now is the time you are actually figuring out what her learning style is—perhaps your child learns best with a hands-on approach and no workbook pages at all! "Math block" could be her self-preservation against confusion, boredom, or simply not being ready yet. Our personal "math block" happened in third grade, and was solved by totally discontinuing our A Beka math and spending some hands-on time with Cuisinaire Rods. Curricula should always be merely a tool and will always be incomplete and imperfect. Your relationship with your child is more important than any recommended workbook, any preferred grade, and any comparison with another family's success. The attitude with which you approach your child and a subject is much more important than your perceived strength in that subject. Make sure that you enjoy learning with her, or make sure that you change (attitude, curricula, or timing).

P.S. I know I'll probably get a hundred irate letters for this, but I personally could never "get" Miquon Math—I bought the 2nd grade and it didn't connect with either of us, so we dropped it—no guilt!

P.P.S. On second thought, those of you who do love Miquon, write me here and I'll forward your letters to Pondering Paula!

Dear Karen,
    I've been impressed by our support group's activities for my

son, but am apprehensive that he will miss out on team sports as
he gets older. Exactly what is offered or can be in this area?
Signed, **WANNABE LIKE MIKE**

Dear Wannabe,

Well, Middle TN (or wherever you live) is the place to be!
We ourselves expressed and heard so many complaints & tears
that our boys would ask to go "back to school" to play sports,
that we found the solution: to not simply provide an alternative
to public/private school teams, but to do it BETTER! The results
of several hard pioneering (sound familiar?) years of efforts are
indeed paying off:

•••Our homeschool swim team posted incredible winning seasons against year-round swim clubs.

•••Our varsity soccer team (with a homeschooled teen for a
coach!) has a 17-3 record for the past 3 years, with at least one
graduate going on to play college soccer.

•••We currently have 4 basketball teams in this area: boys and
girls junior varsity, and boys and girls varsity. Beginning from
scratch (no gym, no uniforms, no alumni money), we recruited
a coach and combined that with devoted kids (willing to practice
hard and work for money for uniforms, referees, and trips) and
dedicated parents (dads to help coach, be on parental boards,
referee, and keep score, and moms to spend hours on the phone
lining up scrimmages, games, gyms, refs, volunteers, and con-
cessions). God has worked tremendously to unite us into an incredibly supportive "family." The caliber of these families willing to sacrifice to build this bridge into the future is phenomenal.
Because these families waited and worked for two years to carve
out a space for homeschoolers out of total non-recognition, our
basketball teams were invited this year to participate in a Christian school league. Our varsity girls ended their local season with
3rd place in the entire conference, and our varsity boys took #1
in the district and #1 in the conference!! If you happen to live
within driving distance of a preferred team sport which has an

opening, you are indeed blessed. (We have many families within the various sports who drive 45 minutes one way to practice, and several hours to games and meets.) But if a team is "closed" (meaning, we'd love to have you, but we already have 10 on the bench), that is the time to remember that there are no shortcuts to success. We have a wonderful baseball program this year and still need a few more dedicated players. We already have competitions for our chess teams. If there is a need or void, pray to see if you are the one to get the ball rolling (sorry). Your child's fondest memories may depend on it. Austin Whitver, our "valedictorian/salutatorian" (one of two National Merit Scholars), spoke at the 1996 graduation. Besides his parents, he thanked his basketball coach and the young man who "talked him into" basketball. Why? Answer: for the friendships, teamwork, self-discipline, and life lessons he learned there. We've had several inquiries regarding football, but are still waiting for someone to run with it (sorry again!). Equipment is rather expensive, but several are looking into corporate sponsorship. At our Summer Conference, we plan on showcasing all the extracurricular activities offered here in Middle TN, including all existing sport teams and all hopeful start-ups.

Dear Karen,
My oldest is entering high school. I have your list of credits for graduation from your handbook, but is there a list anywhere to prepare him for college and scholarships?
Signed, **Prep mom**

Dear Prep,
Colleges are actively pursuing nontraditional students, but it is our job to thoroughly research, carefully document, and forcefully promote how complete our child's education is. The HSLDA publishes a list of over 300 colleges and universities which have accepted homeschoolers. Basically:
1. Pray constantly for God's guidance.

2. Take the PSAT as a 10th grader. (Most guidance counselors at your local public high school will be glad to give you all test applications.)

3. Study the handbook for appropriate college-bound subjects.

4. In the fall of his junior year, take the PSAT again.

5. Throughout his junior year, take the ACT and perhaps the SAT (if your preferred college choice requires it).

6. There are several ACT/SAT prep courses available, or do intense study with the Princeton Review, Barron's, or Gruber editions.

7. Write to colleges to request catalogs and financial aid information, or you can do this on-line.

8. Begin visiting colleges with him. Scholarships can be researched through many volumes at your library, obtained through a computer search business (high cost!), or decided upon with the admissions counselor at your potential college.

What your son needs to qualify for scholarships is:
1. High ACT/SAT scores
2. Honors courses
3. Strong written communication skills
4. Heavy course load as a senior, even if credits for graduation are already met
5. Vocational and academic interests outside of school

In conclusion, do exactly what you did when you first heard of homeschooling:
Pray without ceasing, talk to everyone you can who has successfully done it, and read everything you can get your hands on! Next month—college at home?!?

NOTE: For much more college prep information, see chapter 10 entitled "FIGHT."
Dear Karen,
My daughter, who is 8 years old, has a bad attitude toward school

work. This bad attitude has continued for the past year. I have tried small rewards for good behavior and restrictions on privileges for bad behavior. These options do not seem to affect her attitude. My daughter simply does not believe that she needs any type of schooling. How can I convince her that schooling is imperative and help her improve her attitude?
Signed,
Exasperated Mom

Dear Exasperated Mom,
You didn't share what your daughter's past school experience has been, but my guess is that she has either been in a school system for several years or has been "force-fed" too many workbooks, textbooks, and busy work at home. A child's natural inclination toward learning is wonder, awe, and inquisitiveness. We, as parents, should try to correctly channel that natural wonder into real-life character-building education. Your daughter needs to hear good literature read aloud to her; she needs to have access to paper, markers, colored pencils, and other resources while she's listening; she needs to be involved in meaningful work at home that gives her a significant feeling of belonging; she needs to be encouraged that learning is lifelong, fun, and challenging; she needs to see you both engaged in ongoing learning and ministry and be invited to participate; and she needs to be made aware that "schooling" as you term it, does not consist of workbooks and texts. You sign yourself "Exasperated," and you know that youngsters can sense that exasperation and internalize it. If you can relax and enjoy a unit study on a topic that she is already interested in (say, horses), you'll be amazed at how your approach can free her up to also relax and enjoy you. Of course, a certain routine should be established that is tailored specifically to all the members of your family which is *non*-negotiable. But definitely, take the summer off from what you have attempted so far, and go to libraries, parks, and picnics—all the while, learning.

Dear Karen,
My eighth grader has had a rough year in public school, and I would love to homeschool him next year for some much needed healing. However, we plan on putting him in our local high school for grades ten through twelve. Should this be a problem?
—**Straddling the Fence**

Dear Straddling,
Believe it or not, yes! We had a couple of similar situations here in Middle Tennessee where the local principal has demanded passing of semester tests for each high school subject studied during homeschool. We actually had one student who only wanted to take their senior year at the local high school. The principal actually required them to pass the exam of every semester of every course taken since ninth grade, with absolutely no perusing of any texts or notes. The sad thing is that this is totally within his legal right to require this. Because of this, we now encourage any high schooler who is homeschooling to consider that their only option. Most superintendents and principals are supportive of our choice, but it remains a totally subjective process and one not winnable in court. So, plow ahead, commit to the long haul, and be thankful we have so many high school resources here at MTHEA!

Dear Karen,
Two of my friends, who also have 4-, 5-, or 6-year-olds, have invested quite a bit of money in curricula, and I'm feeling a little underprepared for this next year. What should preschoolers spend most of their time doing?
Signed, **Trying to keep up**

Dear Trying,
The unanimous homeschool moms' cry: AM I DOING ENOUGH? We never totally get beyond that uncertainty, but the ability to relax is reinforced with each year that you realize that you both

are learning, enjoying, and growing to new depths of under-standing of this wonderful God-given privilege. Preschoolers need to be read to—daily. Have plenty of good literature, art resources, and craft supplies available, and YOU be available to help. But do NOT spend much money. Use libraries, parents, friends, and ordinary things at home. Teach yourself how to be creative in simplicity. Stretch your imagination in making every-day happenings a time of learning. Beyond that, a good support group (mostly for *you* at this stage) will be invaluable and an excellent starting point for field trips. Small unit studies can be jump-started from any of these locations (and watch for future columns on recommended field trips).

Dairy
Bakery
TV Stations
Fire Departments
Parks & Rec. Programs
Print Shops
Symphony halls
Museums and science centers
Newspaper
Radio stations
Police Departments
Banks
Drink Bottling companies
City/County Offices (4-H, etc.)
Park Nature Centers
Auto Garages
State Capitol
Airports
Post Offices
Magazine Publishers
Recording Studios (a must in Nashville)
Water Treatment Plants

Manufacturing Plants (Nissan, Saturn, etc.)
Nurseries (the plant kind)
Local Colleges

Dear Karen,
What can I do when I haven't finished what I had hoped to get
done last year, and it's time to start planning a new year?
Signed, **Running Behind**

Dear Running,
We homeschooling moms have an automatic built-in second career: second guessing ourselves! We know we've left things un-
taught (what teacher hasn't?), we realize that the joy of learning
turned like clockwork to almost a drudgery of learning by May,
and we despair of getting "caught up" (WHATEVER THAT
MEANS!). I do hear, however, that your past year was not satisfactory for any of you. If it is that obvious to your children, you
need to be up front with them, apologize for that which was in
your control, and use it to show how wonderful God's grace is
and how His mercies are new every morning. Under the worst
of circumstances, children still are learning. . . how to cope with
trials, how to accept responsibility, how to be independent learners, etc. If bad study habits have become a habit, now is the time
to break it (it will take 3 weeks). Please be certain that you are
setting a good example (tackling your housework, reading those
books worthy of your time, being a careful steward of what the
TV or monitor is bringing into your home, etc.). Plan to start
fresh with a topical study that is of particular interest to your family. Incorporate innovative teaching methods (possible change of
location, using new audiovisuals, letting them research and be
responsible for teaching a portion) and keep your first month or
so exciting. Pray about specific interests and how best to serve
your children. Find another family to help share the load of this
first unit: you'll see how your different giftings complement
each other and keep you motivated. Use family members and

their talents. Remember, we as moms are the climate-controllers in our homes. We need to take this responsibility seriously and yet learn not to take ourselves so seriously!

Dear Karen,
I have 2 children early elementary age who require a lot of one-on-one teaching (i.e., reading and math). I also have a toddler. What do I do with my toddler since she wants to be in the middle of everything all the time? She doesn't take a scheduled nap but does nap at some point in the day. —**Anxious in Middle TN**

Dear Anxious,
I've utilized many options ranging from satisfactory to probably unwise. When my daughter was a toddler, I tried a playpen which I placed in the middle of our schoolroom (since that was also where she wanted to be), filled with new toys and games that she was allowed to play with only at that time. I've also allowed her to roam at free will. This meant that I taught all morning and cleaned up after her all afternoon. One concession, however, was that I had a few low kitchen cabinets filled with plastic and Tupperware which she was allowed to unload and play with while I was teaching one-on-one. I think if I had included her more in reading aloud, coloring, etc., she wouldn't have been quite as demanding of my attention. Let them feel as if they are a real part of your teaching. I actually bought her a desk to go along with the boys'!! And be flexible enough to teach when she does nap.

Dear Karen,
How can we teach our children the concept of ministry when they are most often the recipients of ministry?
Signed, **WORLD REVOLVES AROUND KIDS**

Dear Revolving,
First and foremost, our families need devotion times together

where certain specific ministries are lifted up in prayer. As early as possible, let all the children in on your choices for tithing—let them pray and listen for God's answers and confirmation regarding which ministry (of the many we're all bombarded with!) to support. Set up a pen-pal relationship with your children and one of your local church's missionary families, and discipline them to a regular, ordered way of communicating. Ministry to your local church which involves the whole family is always appreciated. We've "adopted" seniors at a nearby nursing home, and now an elderly man (81 next spring!) lives with us. Many families have taken in unwed mothers and foster children. Remember, however, that this must be a committed calling—not merely something to do to teach the character trait of compassion. Some families plan a summer mission trip; others host retreats and/or hospitality weekends for missionaries on furlough. Take your family down to the Union Rescue Mission to serve meals. Let all your children help make meals for families with newborns, illnesses, or moves. Right now, our whole family is helping paint and wallpaper the farmhouse of another homeschooling family. Look around you for opportunities, no matter how young your children are. Operation World has some great resources for expanding our children's horizons regarding world missions. We plan on featuring a panel on how to involve your children in missions next August at the conference. Your children need to see you both involved in service and ministry projects. If you need any suggestions, we here at MTHEA will welcome your help!

Dear Karen,
I homeschool one child and the other one goes to a local public elementary school. Is there any possible way to balance my time and energy so that when my son gets home, I can give him what he needs? —**Almost Exhausted**

Dear Almost,
Many of us deal with a type of your situation: for example, where

several are at home and an older one(s) is part of a group class or co-op. As we pray for discernment on how each child needs to be individually nurtured, there is no one "cookie-cutter" answer. I do know that it is imperative that we as parents never abdicate our primary responsibility of educating our own children. If we elect to "sub-contract" to others as mentors or teachers, we need to stay as involved as possible as to what is being taught. Be in the classroom with your child, volunteer to chaperone trips, and bring these groups to your house for gatherings. Yes, this takes much extra effort, but with choices and privileges come added responsibility. God is faithful to multiply time and energy—stay attentive to His leading.

Although a few of these columns are a little dated or locale specific, most of the questions posed are timeless. Our excursion toward a homeschool lifestyle can be fraught with insecurity, frustration, and unrealistic expectations. I have found over the years that we all need to be encouraged on this arduous journey. Laughter is a wonderful traveling companion!

KITES

I love kites. I love the whole concept of kites: the simple construction, the creative designs, the joy of the launch, and the freedom of flight. I believe that a kite is a beautiful example of a successful homeschool experience.

As far as the construction of a kite, only the well-balanced will work. If weight is over-emphasized on any one side, it will not carry to heights it was meant to climb. There is actually one entire class of kites known as "tailless kites." They can fly so much higher because they are not carrying any other baggage.

We homeschoolers can so easily become weighted down with worries and concerns that hinder our way. Our baggage can consist of unforgiveness, debt, too many church activities, curricula from past years, and fear. Any of these can weigh us down and keep us from triumphant living in wisdom; we need to choose to drop that which hinders. Jesus loves us enough to set us free from the baggage.

Kites are made to be flown to incredible heights but have to be tethered to the end of a line. At a certain height, the flyer must play out the restraining cord a bit in order to catch the updraft and stay steady. If there is enough resistant wind, the kite will maintain its height and even climb farther. If there is not enough resistance, the kite will jerk and possibly fall. A kite only rises *against* the wind—not with it!

As homeschoolers, we have to be grounded in reality and stability before we attempt to fly solo. Our children will increasingly desire more freedom and privilege, but they must be secure in their foundation. Society continually puts babies in day care, children in front of violent video games, and adolescents in unmonitored computer chat rooms. Children can have some freedom, but we cannot simply let them loose. We, as homeschoolers, have to go *against* this flow. We cannot be afraid of pressure; we need to welcome it as a prelude to flying! We need to live out Ephesians 3:18: "Be rooted and established [grounded] in love," and then we'll have the "power to grasp how wide and deep and long and *high* is the love of Christ." (emphasis mine)

Years ago, the best kites were made from cambric cloth. In our disposable paper-and-plastic world, this sounds strange. It reminds me that if we are not careful, we will substitute the artificial for the best. When I tell audiences about this cambric cloth, of course, they have never heard of it. Much like public education, we've done something cheap and artificial for so long that we don't even know what the best way is!

The kite has been used throughout history, illustrating principles which apply to home education.

1. **Faithful process will ultimately lead to success.**
   Many years ago, Tim and I took all the kids, flew to Detroit, rented a van, and drove the length of Ontario,

Canada, to see Niagara Falls. What an awe-inspiring creation of God! We were almost as amazed at the impossibly high bridge spanning part of the falls. How was that constructed? I was excited to learn that a kite played a major role in its completion. This undertaking began in the mid-1800s to provide a path from this part of Canada to New York. The engineers began the arduous task of building a bridge over the 770-foot falls by flying a simple kite—with a long tail. Onto this tail was tied a heavier string—followed by an even heavier cable—tied then to the heaviest possible cable necessary to hold a railroad track and subsequent trains. Although this track has been replaced by a highway bridge, the humble beginning of a kite string made a strong path for others to follow.

Obviously, our first kindergarten-teaching steps are simple, child-like, and somewhat frail. But little by little, God allows us to see His plan. As we walk closer and closer to Him, He allows us to see farther down His path for us. In the same way, as we disciple our children, we reel out more and more responsibility to them to educate themselves. The question you must ask is: "Who is following behind you on your path, and *have you made it better?*"

2. **Different perspectives give clarity of vision.**
   In the Spanish-American War, kites were used for photography. This proved to be a rather inconspicuous way for a camera to be lifted above the fray for a unique picture of the location of the ground troops. During the Civil War there are records showing the kites were made near Vicksburg in 1863. In 1865, kites were the messengers to take orders over enemy lines in an attempt to entice deserters by offering money for their guns and horses. There was even a request for 10,000 feet of strong kite string.

3. **When we elevate others to places of significance, we affect creativity, discovery, and invention.**
   Kites were the first weather satellites and have been used since 1749. Even though we are more familiar with the balloon as a predecessor to our weather satellite, the balloons had several shortcomings. A free balloon would escape and a tethered balloon could not be adequately controlled. Kites were less expensive and provided much better exposure of the weather instruments.

   God uses many paradoxes to teach us life lessons. He uses the weak, foolish, and the few to bring about amazing miracles that underline that He is in the midst of them. We must show each child that they have been elevated to places of honor in God's eyes, and affirm them with words of their significance to Him.

4. **There can be great value in disaster.**
   Benjamin Franklin is the most well-known kite flyer. Against all odds he chose to use a kite in his famous experiment. History books rarely tell of the incredible danger he faced while experimenting in a lightning storm. He risked disaster in order to follow his inspiration.

   In his later years, Thomas Edison experienced a major fire in his home which destroyed countless documents and unfinished experiments. When asked how he felt about this calamity, he replied, "Disaster? This is fabulous. This allows me to start again from nothing."

As you learn to trust God and soar with Him, remember that it is important to be faithful, to view circumstances from different perspectives, to affirm our children with words of significance, and to see redemption in some disasters. I found the following kite story in an old book several years ago. More than anything this illustrates to me that I want to be the kind of mom who flies kites with my children.

The Day We Flew the Kites

"String!" shouted my brother, bursting into the kitchen. "We need lots more string."

It was Saturday. As always, it was a busy one, for "Six days shalt thou labor and do all thy work" was taken seriously back then. Outside, Father and Mr. Patrick next door were doing chores.

Inside the two houses, Mother and Mrs. Patrick were engaged in spring cleaning. Such a windy March day was ideal for "turning out" clothes closets. Already, woolens flapped on backyard clotheslines.

Somehow the boys had slipped away to the back lot with their kites. Now, even at the risk of having Brother impounded to beat carpets, they had sent him for string. Apparently, there was no limit to the heights to which kites would soar today.

My mother looked at the sitting room, its furniture disordered for a spartan sweeping. Again her eyes wavered toward the window. "Come on, girls! Let's take string to the boys and watch them fly the kites a minute." On the way we met Mrs. Patrick, laughing guiltily, escorted by her girls.

There never was such a day for flying kites! God doesn't make two such days in a century. We played all our fresh twine into the boys' kites, and still they soared. We could hardly distinguish the tiny, orange-colored specks. Now and then we slowly reeled one in, finally bringing it dipping and tugging to earth, for the sheer joy of sending it up again. What a thrill to run with them, to the right, to the left, and see our poor earth-bound movements reflected minutes later in the majestic sky-dance of the kites! We wrote wishes on slips of paper and slipped them over the string. Slowly, irresistibly, they climbed up until they reached the kites. Surely all wishes would be granted.

Even our fathers dropped hoe and hammer and joined us. Our mothers took their turn, laughing like school girls. Their hair blew out their pompadours and curled loose about their cheeks; their gingham aprons whipped about their legs. Mingled with our fun was something akin to awe. The grownups were really playing with us! Once, I looked at mother and thought she looked actually pretty. And her over forty!

We never knew where the hours went that day on the hilltop. There were no hours, just golden breezes. I think we were all beside ourselves. Parents forgot their duty and their dignity. Children forgot their combativeness and small spites. *Perhaps it's like this in the kingdom of heaven*, I thought.

It was growing dark before, drunk with sun and air, we all stumbled sleepily back to the houses. I suppose we had some sort of supper. I suppose there must have been a surface tidying-up, for the house on Sunday looked decorous enough.

The strange thing was, we didn't mention that day afterward. I felt a little embarrassed. Surely none of the others had thrilled to it as deeply as I. I locked the memory up in that deepest part of me where we keep "the things that cannot be and yet they are."

The years went on, then one day I was scurrying about my own kitchen in a city apartment, trying to get some work out of the way while my three-year-old insistently cried her desire to "go park and see ducks."

"I can't go!" I said. "I have this and this to do, and when I'm through I will be too tired to walk that far."

My mother, who was visiting us, looked up from the peas she was shelling. "It's a wonderful day," she offered, "really warm, yet there's a fine fresh breeze. It reminds me of that day we flew kites."

I stopped in my dash in between stove and sink. The locked door flew open and with it a gush of memories. I pulled off my apron. "Come on," I told my little girl. "You're right; it's too good a day to miss."

Another decade passed. We were in the aftermath of a great war. All evening we had been asking our returned soldier, the youngest Patrick boy, about his experiences as a prisoner of war. He had talked freely, but now for a long time he had been silent. What was he thinking of—what dark and dreadful things?

"Say!" a smile twitched his lips. "Do you remember— no, of course you wouldn't. It probably didn't make the impression on you like it did on me."

I hardly dare speak. "Remember what?"

"I used to think of that day a lot in POW camp, when things weren't too good. Do you remember the day we flew the kites?"

Winter came, and the sad duty of a call of condolence on Mrs. Patrick, recently widowed. I dreaded the call. I couldn't imagine Mrs. Patrick facing life alone.

We talked a little of my family and her grandchildren and the changes in the town. Then she was silent, looking down at her lap. I cleared my throat. Now I must say something about her loss... and she would cry.

When she looked up, Mrs. Patrick was smiling. "I was just sitting here thinking," she said. "Henry had such fun that day. Frances, do you remember the day we flew the kites?"

Frances Fowler—submitted by Ruth Rogness

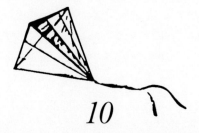

10

Fight

"People who say it cannot be done should quit interrupting those of us who are doing it."

—Banner in Olympics training room

Theodore Roosevelt gave this timeless message in 1917:
"No other success in life—not being President or being wealthy, or going to college or writing a book or anything else—comes up to the success of the man or woman who can feel that they have done their duty, and their children and grandchildren rise up and call them blessed."

The last success strategy and possibly the most important for you as a homeschool mom is to fight. You will need to fight laziness, apathy, being misunderstood, and your own insecurities. Daily there is a war to be fought to give your children the training they need. When you feel beaten down, discouraged, or just plain tired, you need to marshal all available resources to enable you to carry on this glorious challenge. For me that sometimes involves looking back into my history and remembering others who have fought similar fights. My dad was one such soldier.

Bill Smith—yes, that is his real name and he was my dad. The common surname is offset by his unusual middle name: Utley. He was named after a family friend and was the middle child of three. In order for you to understand the strength of his fighting heart, I include here the bulk of a eulogy given at this 81-year-old's funeral by his middle son, Wade:

William Utley Smith was born September 20, 1924, in a very modest home. Despite having a bad leg from contracting polio as a child, he played numerous sports and was a Golden Gloves boxer. After graduating from high school, he worked and saved to go to college where he played basketball and baseball. After college, Dad went into teaching, and he taught and coached for 16 years. During this time, he married Margaret Lipscomb, his wife of over fifty years. They started a family, and as the family grew in size, Dad decided to leave teaching to go to work in real estate in order to better support his family. He led a successful residential real estate company for over thirty years.

In describing Billy Smith, it would not take long for someone to come up with the word "fighter." From fighting for his life as a child, to fighting for his last breath, Bill Smith fought "tooth and nail." He loved sports, and he competed with every ounce he had. He believed that the greatest lessons learned in life were learned in competition. Hard work, discipline, teamwork, respect. Learning to be a good winner and. . . Ok, maybe Dad never learned how to be a good loser. He was a gracious winner, but he was a terrible loser. There are very few people that I know that hated to lose more than my dad. When I played college football, I would come out of the locker room after a loss and my father would still be sitting, up in the stadium all by himself, with his head in his hands agonizing over the loss.

He loved to laugh. He loved a good joke but he was the worst joke teller ever. He would start to tell a joke but could never get to the punch line because he was laughing too hard.

He loved his family. To him, family was everything. Dad was a selfless man whose greatest pride, and truly his mission in life, was to raise his five children. He never brought home his struggles and would drop whatever he was doing to help one of us, even to a fault. He was ALWAYS there for me. I don't mean most of the time, but all the time. He and Mom were committed to raising their children and teaching the tenants of the Christian faith: teaching them respect, obedience, and giving back to their community and family. Dad had a simple but evident faith in his God. Instilled by his mother and realized in his own personal walk with God, my Dad's faith never dealt with heavy doctrine but simply loving God with all of his heart and loving his neighbor.

Dad was one of a small group of men that founded what has become the Middle Tennessee chapter of the Fellowship of Christian Athletes (FCA). He also directed many youth ministries. However, the greatest testament of his faith and the fruit of his labor are in his children. For all five of his children are here today walking in the faith. Indeed, this faith has been nurtured to future generations as not only his children but his grandchildren have made the decision to follow Christ. Even today, we pray for the day when his great-grandson will accept Jesus as his personal savior.

Dad loved his country and this great city in which he lived. Although turned down from all the services in WWII due to his polio, he still served in the State Guard and was so proud of those who had served our country in the military and was deeply moved by their sacrifices.

Love of sports. Love of country. Love of family. Love of God. Not a bad combination. I said at the beginning that this was a celebration and I mean it. Twenty-five years ago, while walking with a friend, Dad suffered a massive heart attack. Miraculously, he survived. Since that night, every day has been a gift of God and he has experienced so many wonderful moments.

Since his quadruple bypass surgery, he saw the last three of his children join the first two in graduating college, two grandchildren graduate from college, his wife receive a master's and doctorate, and one grandson graduate from medical school. Since that time, he experienced the joy of one son playing college football and the truly life-changing, faith-building experience of sending another son off to combat in the Persian Gulf War. He was able to truly enjoy his grandchildren, seven of the eight coming after his heart attack, and even the birth of a great-grandson. I think most of all, about how he was able to grow old with his wife and enjoy her company.

No, today is not a day for sadness. For God not only spared him from death 25 years ago but also 80 years ago when he contracted polio and typhoid fever. Now *that* death would have been sad, for I think of all the people's lives that would not have benefited from and been impacted by my father. The boys and girls that he taught and coached, his family that he loves and molded, the influence he had in the local community, the children with birth defects that he helped through the March of Dimes, the kids who have been influenced through the youth ministries and camps that he directed, those whose lives have been impacted through the local FCA chapter, and the many friends along the way who were drawn to his upbeat, cheerful personality. A perfect man by no means—other than perfect through the grace of Christ Jesus. But nonetheless, a kind and decent man whose life influenced and impacted those far beyond these walls throughout this great community.

Today, we will leave this funeral and life will go on. Meetings. Phone calls. Text messages and ball games. But in the end, our bodies will all end up in an overpriced box like the one in front of you today. It may be four days, four years, or four decades, but we will all be here. I'd ask you to reflect on the following: What are you going to do with the days you have left? Who are you going to influence and what will your impact be? For Bill Smith, he left a great legacy and truly did have "a wonderful life." We'll miss you, Dad, and look forward to seeing you again real soon. You definitely finished strong!

I cannot leave out the fighting spirit on my mom's side of the family. Her ancestor, for whom she is named, was an amazing woman. Margaret Zellner Lipscomb, the night she met her husband-to-be, was wearing a homemade gingham dress and a hat she had personally made from corn shucks. After she married David, she made him a pair of shoes from an old felt hat. She decorated the walls of their home with her own paintings and delicate needlework. She covered the beds with her handmade quilts and used scatter rugs she had made with her own hands. For chairs and couches, she embroidered cushions, and she crocheted doilies for her table. The farm grew the wheat that she husked, washed, and ground with her own hand mill. She personally planted and tended an extensive garden, and even grew peanuts to make peanut butter. Dr. Robert Hooper, in *Crying In The Wilderness* said: "She bore, watched the death of, built a casket for, and buried her only child; raised eleven others in her household; personally maintained two farms in a snake- and savage-infested wilderness—while her husband rode away to save the world."

I share this part of my heritage to recount how my ancestors fought to survive. We should all look into our own family history to fully understand the privilege we have been given today. I venture to say that you will have much more determination to fight for your freedom to homeschool after you study what your own family encountered.

As you read A.W. Tozer, you need to hear his message: Come near to the holy men and women of the past and you will feel the heat of their desire after God. They wrestled and sought for Him every day in every season. Read Tozer's *The Pursuit of God* to challenge you to continue your quest for home education. Many other great men and women in the past recognized the ongoing forging process of suffering. Helen Keller said, "Character cannot be developed in ease and quiet. Only through experiences of trial and suffering can the soul be strengthened, vision cleared, ambition inspired, and success achieved."

Nothing happens to us by accident. I believe setbacks can be God-given challenges sent to change our complacency to passion. So never side-step challenges. Grab the bull by the horns and slap him twice across the face. Remind him that God is in control of you and you are in control of him. Don't get into the habit of celebrating leisure while condemning hard work. It is better to place leisure and labor side by side. Leisure will give margin to your life, while labor will make you productive.

We all know that self-discipline is an ongoing, steady fight.

The hardest time for me to make myself continue to homeschool is the let-down after a hectic Christmas season. Not only are we over-tired and unorganized, but the grey weather and the cold, short days take a toll on me. I have to fight to continue to be consistent—to be joyful.

Much the same way as God shapes me, I am responsible to shape and discipline my children. Some of the ways I shape them is by:

1. Teaching them how to think
   The majority of kids today simply know how to please teachers—not how to think.
2. Stretching the human mind
   It is our job to plant seeds that will bear fruit.
3. Teaching them how to learn
   In our example, we need to perpetuate learning for the rest of our lives. The Bible speaks more about discipline than any other subject. Training involves discipline. We must be available and have a servant's heart. For example, in order to train in orderliness, we need to realize that that same two-year-old who took out all the toys is able to put them all back.

As we are learning to discipline and train our children, it is very important not to push them too much. When Scripture exhorts fathers not to provoke their children to wrath, this means expecting more than they are capable of producing at the time we ask them. Genesis 33 also has an interesting story which relates to being aware of children's limits. Jacob has just described his children as blessings from the Lord. Esau urges them to go forward on a long journey. But Jacob says, "You know that the children are young and tender. . . The animals are nursing their young, and if they are driven hard for even one day, all the animals will die. Please let me move along slowly *at the pace of my children*" (emphasis mine).

Homeschoolers are almost never finished in their tasks. Their fighting spirit seems to say, "This undertaking will always be in process. It will never be finished." Now that we stand on this plateau, I would like you to lift your eyes up to the next pinnacle. We're called to be over these. Do not celebrate overly on this small victory. The mountain we're sent to conquer is yet to be climbed.

Fighting for a Purpose

The hard times in life prove our mettle. I had a glimpse of the man Tim Costello would be when he agreed one summer to sell Bibles door-to-door 200 miles away from home when he was only eighteen! He actually lived on his own, worked 90 hours per week, and got around by hitch-hiking! It was the hardest part of his life and he succeeded in a tremendous way. He conquered fear and loneliness, and learned how to manage all his business and finances. His take-home pay was amazing for a high school senior in one summer, but his business acumen and growth in maturity were astounding. He continued to do this incredibly hard job every summer for the next ten years—and added on team members each year until he set a record at the Southwestern Company for the most successful team in their history! He had to fight through discouragement, fatigue, rejection, and home-sickness. He developed his heart of a fighter walking mile after mile, having door after door slammed in his face. God would use the perseverance he learned during these summers to help him fight through many other obstacles later.

My early personal physical struggles were related to child-birth. When we were expecting our first child, we were so excited to read about and prepare for a natural childbirth. This seemed to be a necessary milestone for me to prove something to myself: was I strong enough to do what I felt was best for my baby?

Most of my other expecting friends were anticipating an epi-dural delivery, but I was not certain that that was healthy for the delivery, so I read everything I could on Lamaze delivery and went to every class session possible.

When it was close to my delivery date, we had an ultrasound as the baby had not fully dropped. The radiologist said he believed the baby was not quite ready to be delivered. However, that night I went into a long labor. After 36 hours of labor and two hours of pushing, it was determined that the baby was too large to be delivered vaginally, so. . . I had an epidural. Tim was banished from the delivery room—and after many "epidural shakes" and being left *alone* for an hour strapped to a cold, steel table, our precious firstborn, William Timothy, was born by Caesarean section. He was almost 9 ½ pounds and perfectly beautiful. The recovery, after essentially having both a natural and a C-section delivery, was rough. That experience emboldened me to research how a birth like that could be avoided the next time. At that period in Nashville history, there were only four doctors who were willing to attempt to deliver a baby vaginally after a previous Caesarean section (called a VBAC). I fought for the decision to be able to labor the way I wanted to—and it was a fight! Most hospitals were against it, the insurance companies termed it high-risk, and family members were doubtful. However, Vanderbilt Hospital and its director of high-risk obstetrics, Dr. Frank Boehm, were the answer to my prayers. For our second baby, we prayed, prepared, and went into "battle" for this baby.

He was three weeks late—and with each passing day, we knew the baby was growing larger and the chance for a repeat Caesarean was growing higher. After a special prayer led by a church friend on Wednesday night, God put me into labor early Thursday morning. Although Dr. Boehm had repeatedly encouraged me that this time I would deliver a "normal, 7 pound" baby, Gilbert Lipscomb was born five hours later—naturally—weighing almost 10 pounds!

This entire period truly made me a fighter in so many ways— the fight to go against the popular culture, the fight for what was best for me and my baby, the fight against the easy way out.

With Tim as my coach, we labored and fought our way through all four pregnancies and deliveries (the last at almost 42!)—and grew stronger together. Little did we realize that it was more preparation for the years to come.

The next hard battle we fought together involved our finances and our marriage—and they were certainly connected. Immaturity, youthful pride, and several bad choices led us both to the brink of financial ruin and to the near dissolution of our marriage. The Lord faithfully sent hope, help, and some of His greatest servants to help us out of the pit we had dug. We would not trade the lessons learned—but discipline is *not* fun! We had to learn to pull together, a process that is still not over.

Practical creeds for our family were shaped during this decade: we would never again pay another new-car payment; we would never again use a charge card; we would place our spouse in his/her intended place of priority in our lives; we would never again attempt to elevate image over relationship (in other words: not just "keep up with the Joneses," but try to surpass the Joneses).

When God had redeemed our relationship, He put a call on our lives to home educate. This was in 1983—when home schooling was illegal in the state of Tennessee! We had read a book that mentioned it and were intrigued by the concept. We knew no one who homeschooled, and certainly there was no one who had graduated from home education. (This, of course, excludes so many great leaders of long ago, including George Patton, Thomas Edison, Pearl Buck, Albert Einstein, Benjamin Franklin, Patrick Henry, George Washington, Thomas Jefferson, James Madison, John Quincy Adams, Abraham Lincoln, Teddy Roosevelt, Stonewall Jackson, Robert E. Lee, Douglas MacArthur, Jonathan Edwards, Dwight L. Moody, and many more.)

Because we are both first-borns and have tremendous stubborn streaks, we decided to not only pursue homeschooling, but to be part of the group who worked downtown at the legislature to legalize home education. We fought hard to make home education legal here in Tennessee. We have seen much progress when convicted Christians commit to work together for a greater cause.

I believe there is much wisdom in chronicling the hardships you face and conquer. Here is a journal entry I wrote when we were going through some amazingly hard times in our marriage and with our finances.

In the beginning, there were two sets of parents. And each prayed for and received their firstborn.
And God said, "This is good."
The parents continued praying for this son and this daughter and nurtured them in the ways of the Lord.
And God said, "This is good."
The boy grew in stature and in wisdom. He learned loyalty in friendships and gained great respect in the world of trade.
And God said, "This is preparation."
The girl grew in happiness and in abundance of friends and learned the value of a sincere smile. And God said, "This is preparation."
And the boy and the girl began a home.
And God said, "This is good."
And God bestowed on them much worldly goods and freedoms to travel to foreign places. The boy and girl believed these material possessions and these freedoms contained much value.
And God said, "Do not be deceived."
Then these freedoms were taken away and replaced with mortgages, loans with interest, and lawsuits. The boy learned to cherish second-hand clothing, and the girl learned to stretch vegetable soup with ketchup.
And God said, "This is necessary."
And God in His infinite wisdom granted gifts of immeasurable value: fathers who made payments, mothers who stocked and re-stocked the pantry, brothers and sisters who lent from their own coffers, and friends who gave of themselves and truly understood.
And God said, "This offering of self is to be treasured above all else."
And the boy and girl learned gratefulness.

God desires fighters to use for His glory: just look at the mighty men and women of His Word! He will use circumstances, trials, promptings, and others to ready us for the battles He has for us. Welcome His teachings and His discipline. Chronicle His faithfulness during those times.

Besides the initial decision to homeschool, your next biggest battle to fight will be that of teaching high school. This is the time to re-commit and re-adjust your priorities. It will require all your energy, patience, dedication, and creativity to continue.

Preparing for Your Children's College

Although it may seem strange to see college prep material in a chapter entitled "Fight," this is an apt title. The road through high school is incredibly difficult—and you *and* your child must fight against the natural inclination to have them in school and let the system complete your job. In addition to the battle inherent in the day-to-day discipline of succeeding in advanced-level classes, there is the additional fight that must be waged in the arduous college admissions process. This chapter provides a year-by-year general guideline that will aid you on the road to high school graduation, college selection and admission, and the fight for potential scholarships.

As your child is entering high school, there is much preparation for both of you. You are examining online courses, local one-day tutorials, and community college options for later. Make them responsible for beginning to learn the art of budgeting time, keeping records and portfolios intact, and researching the merits of potential classes.

Freshmen Year

In their freshmen year, it is important that you know the credit requirements of the church-related school or institution where you are registered. You *are* allowed to count three credits before ninth grade, but usually this is not a great option. For example, even if your child is able to handle Algebra I in seventh grade, there will be years before he can score well on his ACT/ SAT tests. Algebra is one of many incremental studies intended to lead up to their later high school years when they are finally able to take college admissions tests. Proceed cautiously in your accounting of credits and know that there are prerequisites for certain high school classes.

Ninth grade is the year to start a language, if you have not already done so. The reasoning behind this is that it gives your child plenty of time to take not only the required two years of language, but an additional third or fourth year, or two years of an additional language. The world we live in will require our children to be much more versed in other cultures than we were. Also, on a high school transcript, it is much more impressive to list several years in a language, or two or more languages. You must realize that our European (and other nations) cousins master three or more languages at a minimum, and our children will be in competition later with these students.

In our case, our oldest knew that he wanted to go into medicine, so we chose Latin for his language, completing three years of it. Our second son was very involved at that time in Spanish-speaking missions, so I had a tutor teach him two years of Spanish. Our next child loved the French language (thankfully I could teach that!), and we not only completed three years of it, but she lived in France and worked with a church there for five weeks one summer. I personally love Latin as a springboard to any other language.

Be very open to allowing your children to pick the language that will best work for them. Pray often, and have them pray. Only God knows what He has planned for them.

Ninth grade is also the year to begin Algebra I. Here in Tennessee, there is a new law requiring four years of mathematics in high school. Research how your particular curriculum or tutor presents the various math courses: Algebra I and II, Geometry, Trigonometry, and Calculus.

Many high school scope and sequence lists have a particular order of math courses and sciences they deem most efficient. Our daughter actually took her sciences "backward" according to their calculations. She took physics, chemistry, and then biology—but it worked in her schedule. As in all things, think outside the box.

As I am gearing this entire section toward preparation for college, I will also pass on many helpful strategies for procuring college scholarships. Even though the top homeschoolers are being recruited by the nation's best universities, there is still much discrimination in the scholarship arena for home educated students. For example, a criterion of some of the top monetary awards given to public and private school students is on the basis of their school and club involvement. This puts homeschoolers at a distinct disadvantage—but there are ways to level the playing field.

In the ninth grade, it is important to assess your child's interests, as well as all available opportunities, and join a club. For many of you reading this, this might involve *starting* a club based on your child's interests. In addition to existing Scouts and 4-H, other possibilities include drama clubs, chess clubs, photography clubs, equestrian groups, language clubs, debate clubs, and political, civic, and ecological organizations.

Believe it or not, our reason for starting or joining a club will be for the leadership potential and for the immense scholarship opportunities given to those in clubs for several years. In school, these clubs typically have an adult sponsor, have quarterly meetings, and conduct an activity once a semester. There may or may not be dues, a secretary taking minutes, and a yearbook picture. Each club makes up its own rules and reason for being. That is why it is not artificial to create a club for homeschoolers simply for the future potential for scholarships. The end is not just membership—the end is the leadership position attained in that particular club or organization. Scholarship committees are looking for not only involvement, but years of involvement resulting in titles of leadership. This may seem contrived, but it is important to begin in the ninth grade as a member, progress as a sophomore to a position of leadership, and end as a junior in the role of VP or president. You must keep careful records of all leadership positions in these clubs or extracurricular organizations.

Scholarship committees are also very interested in volunteer work. Again, record keeping is vital. You may think you will remember every child's participation in each neighborhood clean-up, soup kitchen, or 5K, but you may not. Top scholarships are awarded on the basis of academic excellence, display of leadership, volunteer experience, and overall interview. Colleges are looking for assets to their student body and campus, and it is up to you to present your child as accomplished.

Sophomore Year

In October of your child's sophomore year, have them take their first PSAT test (you might have to register for this in September). This is not a preliminary SAT, but a vehicle to determine and award the National Merit Scholarship. This is actually a pre-test during your sophomore year. The award and scholarship are given for the test scores recorded in their junior year. There is no actual strategy to study for this—just get plenty of sleep the night before and a good breakfast. You may register and take this test as part of your church-related school or at your local public high school. This scholarship is what I term "free money"—actually given on the basis of accrued information and how well your student takes tests.

Sophomore year your child will need to take Algebra II. Your overall strategy is to complete Algebra I and II before your junior year when you take chemistry. This pacing of classes is most efficient to the timing of the college admissions tests.

Sometime during your sophomore year, you may want to look into preparing for your first ACT, which will be in the spring. Most cities have prep courses, but be advised that some are very expensive. You may also buy the Princeton ACT or SAT review book at your local bookstore. You must register weeks in advance. When you first register, you will be amazed at the length of the application. On this initial one, your student will complete a personal inventory of career choices. This seems silly at the time, but you will complete this part only once, and it could be a good indicator of your child's vocational interests. From this point onward until graduation, your registration process will take minimal time. Take your first ACT test in the spring.

Junior Year

In October of your child's junior year, he will take the official PSAT for the National Merit Scholarship. Your child, having completed Algebra II, is now ready for chemistry. A lab is important, so you may have to be creative. If your area tutorial does not have one, you may check into a local university or community college. We sat down with the vice president and head of the chemistry department of a wonderful university with a great pre-med department. We "sold" them on the idea that if they would set up a chemistry lab for our homeschoolers in their college chemistry department, those students would be exposed to their facilities and might easily want to attend there upon graduation. It truly was a "win-win" situation. This program still continues eleven years later!

Continue encouraging greater leadership positions in all extracurricular activities. This includes sports. Our sons were assistant coaches for our varsity soccer team because we adults did not grow up with, and therefore didn't understand, all the technicalities of that sport.

Senior Year

If you are still not pleased with your child's score, you may have him take the ACT one last time during the fall of his senior year. There is really no point to take it the second semester because most universities will have already begun committing scholarship money by then. There is some talk as to colleges not appreciating the number of times the tests are taken, but we have seen nothing substantial to that rumor. You may take the test four or more times.

The spring semester will be full of writing essays, completing applications, and visiting universities. Know that *you* are your child's greatest advocate, and there is nothing wrong with notifying one college admissions head with the offers your child has received from other colleges. Try to meet with the chairman of the department and never with the newly graduated employee who actually has little authority to grant much scholarship aid.

If you are going through extremely difficult circumstances, I would recommend reading Fox's *Book of Martyrs*. The perspective you gain could be life changing. Years ago in a Christian magazine, I read the following paragraph by Stephen W. Griffin about the heart of the martyrs and the fight they fought:

> Fires didn't make the martyrs, the fires just revealed them. When men and women gave their lives for what they believed, the act of sacrifice didn't change them. Instead, it simply revealed what they were all along. The real fire was not the fire that consumed their bodies—the real fire was the one which burned in their hearts—fueled by an abiding and genuine courage.

Prayer for Parents:

I pray that I may let my child live his own life and not the one I wish I had lived. Guard me against burdening him with doing what I failed to do. Help me to see his missteps today in perspective against the long road he must travel. Grant me the grace to be patient with his slow pace.

Give me the wisdom to know when to smile at the small mischiefs of his age and when to show firmness against the impulses which he fears and cannot handle. Help me to hear the anguish in his heart through the din of angry words or across the gulf of brooding silence. And having heard, grant me the ability to bridge the gap between us with understanding.

I pray that I may raise my voice more in joy at what he is, than vexation at what he is not, so that each day he may grow in sureness of himself. Help me to regard him with genuine affection so he will feel affection for others. Then give me the strength, oh Lord, to free him so he can move strongly on his way.

My favorite translation of Ephesians 3:20 comes from the Amplified version: "Expect great things from God. Believe that He is able to do superabundantly far over and above and beyond all that we dare ask or think—infinitely beyond our highest prayers, desires, thoughts, hopes, or dreams, according to His power which is at work in us."

"If we work on marble, it will perish . . . brass, time will efface it. If we rear temples, they will crumble into dust; but if we work upon immortal minds and instill in them just principles, we are then engraving upon that tablet that which no time will efface—but will brighten and brighten to all eternity."

—Daniel Webster

As you fight, pray, and instill these ten timeless principles, you can indeed expect God to bless your endeavor in His beautifully creative ways. The joys you will experience as you allow Him to teach you the art of kite-flying as it pertains to teaching your children will overwhelm you. You will soar in His timing— with His strength—to unimaginable heights.

> An enterprising young mom of a six-year-old boy who had just begun taking piano lessons heard of an upcoming concert. The world-famous composer Paderewski was giving a concert at the symphony hall in their town. This mom not only wanted to expose her son to grand society, but especially to birth a vision in her son of his potential future as a pianist. The family bought

front-row tickets and dressed formally for the evening out.

While waiting for the maestro to come out onto the stage, the dad and mom turned around in their seats and began visiting with their other socialite friends. The little boy, bored and fidgeting, suddenly saw the baby grand piano steps away from him. He left his seat, sat down at the bench, and began playing his newly learned piece entitled "Chopsticks."

The refined crowd became indignant that their elegant evening was being ruined by a simple little boy and his silly little piece. Cries of "What is he doing?" and "Sit down!" were heard by his shocked parents. However, before they could jump up to retrieve him, something extraordinary happened. Paderewski, who had been watching from backstage, calmly and elegantly came and sat by the boy on the piano bench. He placed his hands around the boy's quivering fingers and added a beautiful symphonic harmony to the child-like plinking. All the while, he kept whispering to the boy: "Don't give up. Keep playing." And the resulting song was a true masterpiece.

This illustration is a pale allegory of how God helps me as I homeschool. I feel that my "playing" is simple—rudimentary—even silly at times. And it seems that there will never be a masterpiece if I have anything to do with it. But when I'm tempted to give up, I feel God is surrounding me with His able hands and turning my elementary plinking into a gorgeous symphony of His design while He whispers to me, "Don't give up. Keep playing." And I do.

LaVergne, TN USA
24 August 2009
155735LV00005B/1/P